WPA BUILDINGS

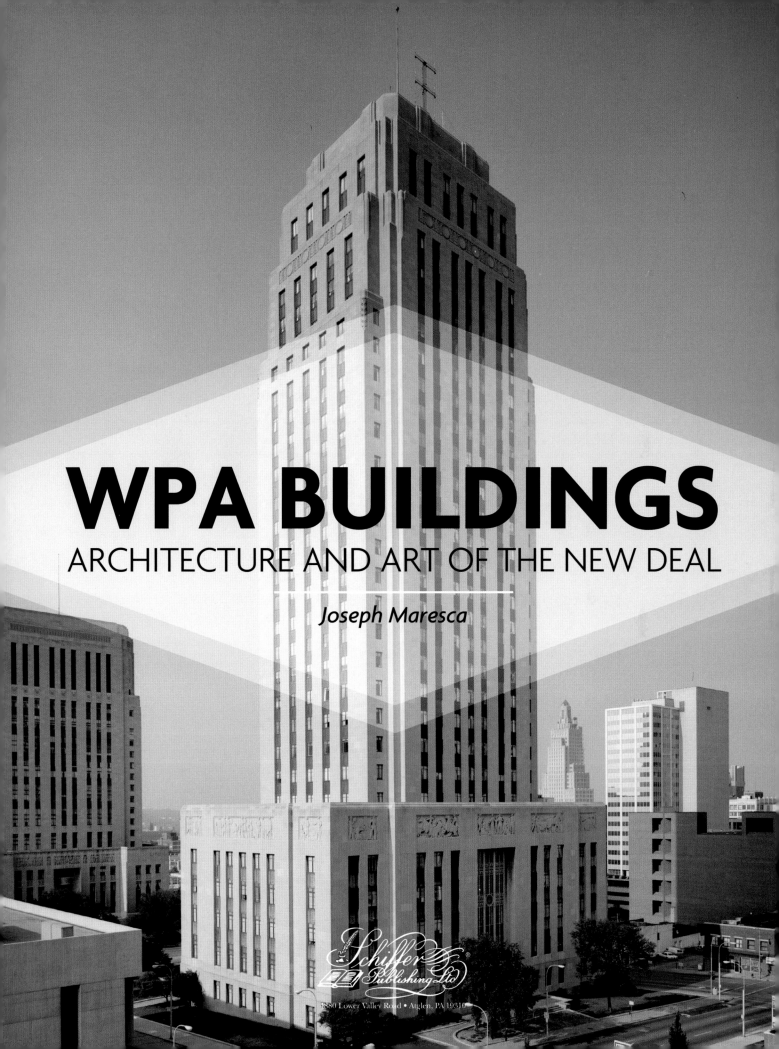

WPA BUILDINGS

ARCHITECTURE AND ART OF THE NEW DEAL

Joseph Maresca

Schiffer Publishing Ltd

4880 Lower Valley Road • Atglen, PA 19310

Cover design by Molly Shields
Interior design by Matt Goodman
Type set in Agenda & Minion

ISBN: 978-0-7643-5211-9
Printed in China

Published by Schiffer Publishing, Ltd.
4880 Lower Valley Road
Atglen, PA 19310
Phone: (610) 593-1777; Fax: (610) 593-2002
E-mail: Info@schifferbooks.com
Web: www.schifferbooks.com

For our complete selection of fine books on this and related subjects, please visit our website at www.schifferbooks.com. You may also write for a free catalog.

Schiffer Publishing's titles are available at special discounts for bulk purchases for sales promotions or premiums. Special editions, including personalized covers, corporate imprints, and excerpts, can be created in large quantities for special needs. For more information, contact the publisher.

We are always looking for people to write books on new and related subjects. If you have an idea for a book, please contact us at proposals@schifferbooks.com.

Contents

Introduction: Love at First Sight
First Impressions Last Forever

Where I grew up, in Brooklyn, New York, the few large buildings in the neighborhood were either churches or theaters—all built to impress, very ornate, and in the case of the theater, over-the-top baroque (think: Angkor Wat).

Then came a major revelation: One day my mother took me to a large building that was like nothing I had ever seen before. It was the local branch of a large bank, the Lincoln Savings Bank, and it was . . . gasp! . . . so impressively different—modern!

Stepping inside, almost everything struck me at once. I could smell the freshly polished brass and bronze and drink in the wonderful color of the polished marble walls, all lit by huge square windows that were not stained glass. It seemed the entire history of money was portrayed in a mural around the walls, in earthy resonant tones. Rising through this impressive brilliance were smoothly fluted columns—not classical, as they had no tops or bottoms—soaring up to a beautifully illuminated golden ceiling.

If ever there were a place to entrust with my greatest treasure—my first savings account—I had found it. This building struck a powerful chord in me, and so began my love affair with the "modern," which has grown steadily since and led me to the work of this book. It was my desire to define this orphaned art form and place it into a context, in comparison to the more visually abundant art moderne. It is important to clarify how this style set itself apart visually and emotionally from the rest of the grid.

During the period between the two great wars, something had to be done to show the American people that there was still something civic to put their faith in—something with the kind of solidity that banks were known for before the crash of the Depression. The municipal center of the town needed to project strength and endurance as America faced great financial challenges. And endure the newly con-

structed city buildings did, which is how this book came to be.

In my inquiries into the architecture of the deco era, there was very little if anything that touched on the subject of the era's federal buildings. Little information was available about the buildings' distinctive use and visual cues. While it was relatively easy to find information on the paintings and other artwork of the Depression years, there was not much discussion of the civic architecture that emerged with the New Deal. I felt there was a need to connect the dots so a picture of the buildings' style could be developed and shown in relation to the other moderne works of architecture

that developed concurrently. I soon discovered the far-ranging locations in which some of the best-preserved examples resided, and through the Library of Congress and its architectural archives was able to find photographs of how these buildings looked when crisp and new. These vintage prints, along with photographs from the Carole Highsmith archive—also housed at the congressional library—proved to be the greatest source of visual documentation.

All the buildings I chose to include in this book were selected for what I felt were their aesthetic qualities and exemplary designs. Additionally, all of these beautiful buildings of the period still function, though

in some cases they have been repurposed for new use. The buildings selected extend across the broad expanse of America, so interested readers can perhaps see these buildings today in the context of their own urban centers.

My hope is that readers will see the beauty I saw in my early years and that I continue to celebrate today with this book.

Chapter One: WPA Style
Alive and Well Everywhere in America

US Post Office, Courthouse, and Custom House, Key West, Florida, 1933, façade of local coquina coral stone. A ubiquitous style for all climates. No red tile roof; only the palms give a hint to the geographic location of the building.

There it stands, four-square and forward-looking, and unashamedly modern in design. In what was then one of the furthest outposts of the Federal Postal System—Key West, Florida—sits a streamlined yet stolid structure that is the US Post Office, Courthouse, and Custom House of 1933. The discreet and elegant building's exterior is of a local coral stone called coquina, which ties it instantly to its locus. But stylistically, it is only the surrounding palm trees that give one any hint of where the building might be.

The building is a fine example of what we have come to understand as WPA style. It was a style that stretched from coast to coast, as the New Deal called for an abundance of new civic buildings, all constructed as federal projects with the goal of putting the unemployed back to work. The WPA, created in 1935 as the Works Progress Administration, was the largest of the New Deal agencies. It was a work-relief program that ultimately gave jobs to more than 8.5 million people.

But the WPA was much more than a jobs program. The program stabilized the country and gave the public a feeling of pulling through the challenges of the economic crisis and getting on with business. Its 85,000 civic buildings became the public face of America. The large and important buildings defined the era and its distinctive style.

Driving across America today, one can still see, if one looks closely, in every city, large and small, certain structures and sculptural embellishments that stand out with their crisp, imposing stonework and distinguished but reserved decoration. These WPA-created federal courthouses and post offices strike one immediately as civic buildings—public structures of importance. With their symbolic carvings and motifs, they proudly announce that the American government has arrived as a steady presence—the eagle had landed. Indeed, with their carved reliefs and solidly calm appearance, their rows of tall glass and bronze windows, they exude a sense of permanence. All of this public work cost, in the end, $11 billion but the results have been long lasting. One has but to glance today at the federal buildings in

Municipal Center, Kansas City, Missouri, 1934, main façade. This massive building shows the conventions of the WPA style and makes a powerful first impression.

US Post Office and Courthouse, Galveston, Texas, 1937, eagle over door frame. The symbol of our democracy , the bald eagle, was used constantly throughout the WPA era to denote a federal or civic structure.

Federal Building and US Courthouse, Binghamton, New York, 1935, façade. This building shows a monolithic power. This style of early minimalism made a powerful statement about the civic nature of the building, once represented by the neoclassical column.

places like Key West or Kansas City, Missouri, or Binghamton, New York, to be aware of their continuing sense of authority and civic duty.

These buildings, ubiquitous across the American landscape, clearly show how the New Deal and its programs were taken seriously into the American heart and identity. And this sense of American identity is present in and on almost every federal project of the period, including the iconic reliefs on the Federal Trade Commission Building in Washington that capture, in stone and for eternity, the spirit of the American worker.

Form Follows Function

In March of 1933 President Franklin D. Roosevelt took the oath of office with the country in a state of extreme economic depression. The toll taken in every segment of society was huge. The hope the new administration offered the nation took the form of a powerful set of new ideas, including a series of federally funded programs, among them the Civilian Conservation Corps, created in 1933, which put unemployed young men to work building parks and roadways and more. The Public Works Administration (PWA) was also formed in 1933. Created under the National Industrial Recovery Act, the PWA gave money for the planning and construction of large-scale building projects.

The 1926 Public Buildings Act had allowed the government to hire private architects to design federal buildings. The act led to an era of robust construction, all completed under the Supervising Architect's Office of the Treasury Department.

The number of public buildings constructed in the '30s continued to rise dramatically under the direction of the New Deal. It was a huge undertaking and takeover in 1933 and one that would have been impossible without the progressive thinking of men such as Harry Hopkins and Harold Ickes, to name but two of the most ardent members of the president's inner circle. Hopkins directed the WPA while Ickes was at the head of the PWA.

The public buildings and civic architecture in the period between the wars had a distinct and decidedly formulaic look that set them apart from their neighbors.

Some called this new form of civic building "WPA moderne" or "PWA moderne" or "stripped classical modern." Instead of rows of classical Corinthian or Ionic columns, the new buildings had angular piers, stripped of decoration to emphasize

Federal Trade Commission Building (originally, Apex Building), Washington, DC, 1938, carving at entrance.
The WPA in stone—the iconic and idealized worker of the New Deal.

the play of light and dark upon the façade. Neoclassic architecture, in the US, came to be associated with the public sphere, and these buildings, with their strong verticals and sculpted massing, became a familiar template.

Architecture, one of the most public of arts, became a form of propaganda. From federal courthouses to city halls, the marbled steadfastness of these structures stood as a symbol for the WPA and the American stability it was at work to promote and maintain. By combining simplified forms with quasi-classical columns, the style made a singular strong impression on the street.

Mixed with the aesthetic conservatism of the times, this hybrid of spare and simplified form, married to the modernity of the earlier art deco period, managed to provide a visual remedy for the public's need for a sense of security. The New Deal's civic soundness, expressed in quality materials and streamlined space, used the familiar to ameliorate the emotional effects of the Great Depression on the nation.

While most of these buildings were constructed between 1929 and 1941, their roots could be traced to earlier designs, many formulated by the architect Paul Cret, whose work set the paradigm for civic American architecture. (Read more about Cret and his work in chapter five.)

The Federal Reserve Building in Washington, DC, designed by Cret, and built from 1936 to 1937, influenced much of the civic design of the period. Giant piers

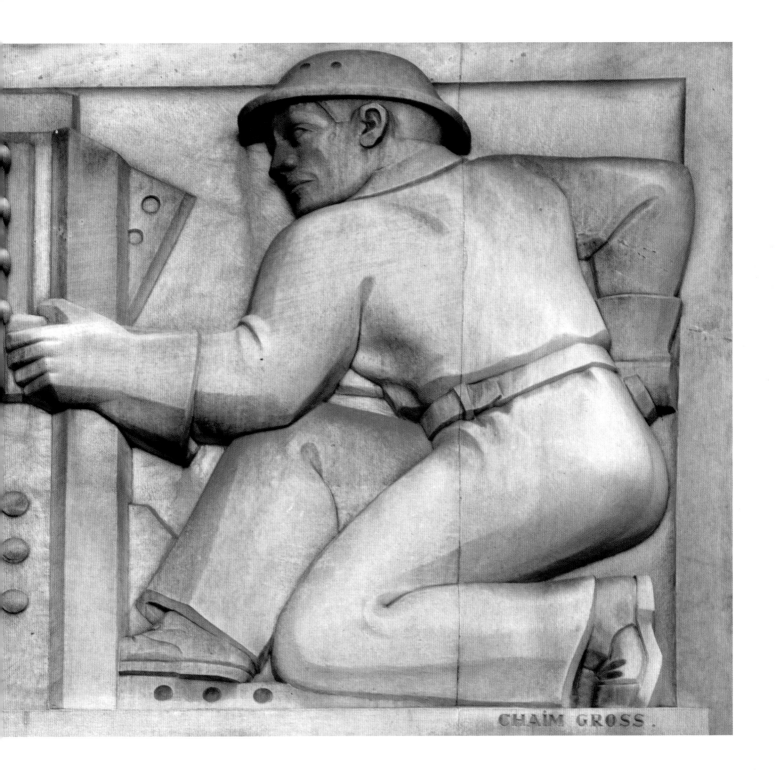

CHAIM GROSS.

without fluting or decoration replaced the traditional idea of a portico. A series of monolithic angular pilasters project from the central bay and create a grand entrance.

The Detroit, Michigan, and the Binghamton, New York, federal courts, constructed in 1934 and 1935, respectively, show two of the most often used conventions—subtle, fluted verticals, projecting slightly from the wall plane as columns; or the plain angular pilaster or pier. These became the architectural constants for the period. Both remind the viewer of their classical antecedents without being direct historical imitations.

Then, as now, the feeling is unique and uniquely American. Though we may not see these as modern today, they were once the epitome of the new, and they still remain distinct from other civic buildings.

The interiors of these buildings were also designed to inspire a sense of dignity through costly but restrained use of materials and subtle but distinctive motifs.

Where there were paintings or murals, they were usually regionalist.

The interiors are unmistakable as space for the public, and at times decidedly theatrical, as in the city hall at Saint Paul, Minnesota.

The public space follows an explicit formula consisting of a lobby, usually double height, connected to a long hall that would serve as space for a post office or courts. As many of the buildings supported judicial and other federal offices, this

Federal Reserve Building, Washington, DC, 1934, approach. This building served as the model for many that followed it.

Decorative grille, 1933. The quality of detail is extremely high in this typical decorative grille.

Federal Building and US Courthouse, Peoria, Illinois, 1938, eagle. A stylized stab at the geometric trend in sculpture and one of the many interpretations of the democratic symbol.

long gallery usually connected to a corresponding lobby for judicial services. Clad in various shades of marble with terrazzo inlaid floors and illuminated by pendant and indirect lighting, the standard for all civic architecture was set, and these interiors still evoke a sense of wonder. The extravagant visual delights contrast perfectly with our sense of the sparseness of "modern."

These civic buildings remain, for the most part, as they were when they first opened, and have been maintained regardless of changing tastes and governments. Some have been transferred by the GSA (General Services Administration) to other institutions with the idea of keeping the historic quality of the building viable, as in Sioux City, Iowa, where renovations in the late 20th century expanded court facilities after the postal services moved to a new building.

The New Deal's New Feel

President Franklin D. Roosevelt and the New Deal made good use of art and design to help create a new picture of America. This new style was first encountered by the president in Chicago, the home of American modern architecture. At the 1933 Century of Progress Exposition, FDR stated clearly that he liked the new buildings and indeed would like to see more of them. With those words he sanctioned and un-

Joel W. Solomon Federal Courthouse, Chattanooga, Tennessee, 1933, façade. This is arguably the most elegantly conceived of the era's federal buildings.

equivocally gave approval for the "new."

A man of the people, but also a man of a distinct upper socio-economic class, Roosevelt, through his background and education, was knowledgeable in the tenets of art and design.

Though conservative in his personal taste, FDR realized that the New Deal had to look *new*. Thus, the moderne was given a green light to be a part of the overall vision. The streamlined but solid styling, modern and user-friendly in the service

Robert A. Grant Federal Building and US Courthouse, South Bend, Indiana, 1933. This exterior shows a subtle shift to the modern in its successful reference to the colonnade of classic columns that would have been used ten years earlier.

of the federal government, blossomed over the next ten years as the face of the new federal works projects.

Through their vast construction projects, a new art and a new architecture entered the American spirit. With the New Deal, as part of its determination to create jobs, came the largest commitment to the arts ever undertaken in our history. These programs put food on the table and paint on the palate. Structures that would house new government agencies dedicated to fulfill this promise were built. Teams of artists and architects worked together to

crystallize a vision of the new, in concrete and marble.

FDR sought an image that was easily identified and understood as forward looking and hopeful—an image that was monumental and publicly scaled.

Civic art and architecture had lain moribund in between styles; one foot in the old world with its classical vistas, and the other on untried soil. This made for some ungainly and confused public buildings. One example is 1933's Trenton, New Jersey, Federal Building, too monumental and too industrial looking to be taken for a new

civic style. The hints are there—simplified pilasters, hardly more than grooved piers, try to make us think "column." The new simplified forms becoming more public were not yet easily handled nor completely understood. The New Deal would bring this new vision into focus.

The country was ready for, and about to embark on, a new direction, socially and politically, and film would play a huge role. Hollywood, as well as European films, began to shape our view of the modern. The buildings were a new experience for many, worldwide, and spoke visually of the

stability the government wanted to telegraph home to the populace; they were monuments of public pride. The message that America the Beautiful was in place and intact sailed across the nation's consciousness.

Just as in the grand movie palaces of the era, with their emphasis on a transcendent experience, a certain emotional chord was touched by these civic spaces of the WPA period. One felt that sense of importance and permanence.

Saint Paul City Hall, in terms of pure theatrics, could hold its own with Radio City Music Hall or Oakland Paramount theater for sheer splendor of the perpendicular kind, though with one subtle difference. In the federal building lobby, the visual connection was predominantly a male one and usually an example of manpower and strength at work. The movie palace of its day was geared to the feminine and thus put less emphasis on power and more on pulchritude. Whatever the mode of expression, the theme was invariably a modern and oftentimes streamlined one.

Perhaps one reason that the concept of abstract did not take hold in America, as it did in Europe, was its tendency to dehumanize. The New Deal, aware of where the bombastic gigantisms of Germany would lead, would happily forego any sense of bullying. The American modernity was meant to inspire, rather than intimidate.

One of the early and important aspects of these commissions was the decoration, in murals, of the new Department of the Interior building, which was to be a showcase for contemporary American art.

Style is something defined by the era, or time frame, in which it was made. For example, art deco, as we know it now, did not acquire that name until the 1960s. The new FDR administration had no interest in looking to past styles for an identity. The New Deal was to be a new visual expression of itself. The buildings and spaces were constructed with the aim of not only em-

Clarkson S. Fisher US Courthouse, Trenton, New Jersey, 1933, façade, showing fluted piers. Though the column might have given way to the pier, the fluting or vertical indents remained as strong reminders of the form's classic antecedents as well as the civic nature of the building.

Clarkson S. Fisher US Courthouse, Trenton, New Jersey, 1933, side view. This building with many classic details, including great interior murals, is a worthy WPA work.

Oakland Paramount Theatre, Oakland, California, 1928, view of the lobby. Classic art deco at its unrestrained height. By the time of the WPA, the public was familiar with the lighting and décor of the high art deco style from their exposure to the various forms of the cinema.

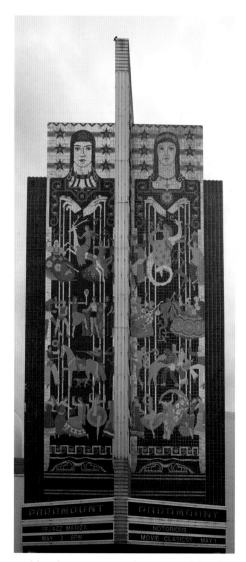

Oakland Paramount Theatre, Oakland, California, 1928, exterior decoration.
A beautiful example of the exuberant art moderne style at the cinema.

E. Ross Adair Federal Building & US Courthouse, Fort Wayne, Indiana, 1932, façade. An example of a severe transitional—still classic in its detail though stripped and streamlined, the building has a certain stiffness that makes it feel slightly uncomfortable in its moderne trappings.

ployment, but also an edification of the national ideal. The spacious interiors were different from anything of the preceding generation. The purpose of a lobby, for example, indeed for the entire building, was to be a stand-in for the government, and to exemplify, in marble and paint, the changes the New Deal had so carefully been implementing.

During the prosperous '20s, and even into the start of the Depression, the decorative and colorful was part of the architectural scene in America. You can see this in 1933's John W. McCormack Post Office and Courthouse in Boston, where the Jazz Age skyscraper has been used as a billboard for "civic virtue," albeit with a jazzy look to it. With colored marble and elaborate grilles and elevator doors, everything was

open for decoration, and design flourished, sometimes like an overgrown garden. The lobbies of many large private buildings, where the style was at its most rich, were transformed into fantastic and colorful spaces. Lightning bolts of bronze and nickel zig-zagged across ceilings, while walls were incised to expose jungles of ornament.

No matter how much the influence of Europe, and especially France, might permeate the artistic sensibilities of our designers and architects, the style that evolved here in the States, now known as art deco, was uniquely American. In cities all across the country, the new style evolved until the party ended in 1929.

But by 1933, America was in a state of flux. Art deco's exuberance was soon left behind for a less fussy version of the classical order. Often translated to new materials such as aluminum and monometal, it become the standard in civic architecture. More straight-edged and angular, this rigid style soon softened to a less sharply defined look, where the edges were softened by increments and the columns were less pronounced.

Fine examples of the new style include the Foley Courthouse in Albany, New York, 1933, and the Philadelphia Federal Reserve Bank of 1935. These, along with the Kansas City, Missouri, City Hall , a high-rise ver-

sion, are exemplary structures in the particular type of reduced classicism that was to be found in most WPA buildings. In the lobby of the Kansas City Hall, rare marbles and simplified lighting give the lobby a modern but still familiar feeing.

In Kansas City, indirect light illuminates the plainer walls and arched ceiling of the cross-shaped, double-height space, while pendant lights of bronze and glass add further scale to the lofty space.

These buildings were built after the Depression hit, but the commissions and materials were ordered before. Hence the seeming excess of marble and the hours of labor of the stonemasons were already in the works. What evolved became a cost-effective means of grandeur, a needed boost to the local economy, and an aesthetic landmark. The blend produced the stripped classic moderne that we identify today as WPA.

Lost and Found

In the decades following the Second World War, these buildings became mostly overlooked, as an elite aesthetic developed that instead embraced glass and steel. In historical surveys and architectural histories, the WPA-style buildings were usually lumped under the catch-all title of art deco,

City Hall, Kansas City, Missouri, 1937, tower. A fine example of the civic tower—modern but easily seen as public. The mass of the building is still dominant to its upward thrust.

City Hall, Kansas City, Missouri, 1937, lobby. Subdued modernism, with luxurious materials and lots of space.

City Hall, Kansas City, Missouri, 1937, lobby. Beautiful materials and an interesting use of spatial divisions by using the mezzanine and cross-shaped plan.

but of a certain type—with less jazz and more sobriety. They lacked the sexiness of the contemporary skyscraper for these mid-century historians of style.

But there now is a renewed interest in the historical importance of the civic architecture of the Depression. And while some buildings have been lost, elements of them have managed to be preserved. For example, the Grand Rapids Civic Auditorium, a 1932 neoclassical building, was replaced by a new facility next door. Here, the builders were able to demolish the interior of the auditorium and reconstruct it, joining it with the new convention center. Despite the gutting of the building, the original entrance façade of the auditorium was spared and restored.

Just as the art that once graced—and in some cases still covers—some of the walls is being revalued, so too is the architecture and design of the era. It is no longer seen as an architectural blunder but an offshoot of modernism in America—federal moderne. Here was a new style that could be easily adapted to both the horizontal lines of the prairie and the verticality of towers then beginning to rise in many of the smaller cities.

Chapter Two: The Evolution of New Deal Style
From Zig-Zag Exuberance to Streamlined Fortress

Federal Courthouse (William Kenzo Nakamura United States Courthouse), Seattle, Washington, 1940, lobby. This sort of simplified dignity was more common towards the end of the WPA era.

Opposite Page: John W. McCormack Post Office & Courthouse, Boston, 1933, façade. Another tower type, clean but with more mass than the Kansas City City Hall.

By the 1930s the exuberance had dimmed, and the high art deco of the '20s was morphing into a new and more austere form, moving from the zig-zag modern and toward a more reserved version of itself. More streamlined and less decorated, it would be a shift to the spare, fit to the times.

In the lobby of the William R. Cotter Federal Building in Hartford, Connecticut, 1933, or Seattle's US Courthouse of 1940, we see the shape of things to come, in their similarities to a fortress.

For the most part, the '30s were a transitional time, as the style gradually shifted

US Post Office and Courthouse, Galveston, Texas, 1937, façade. Simplicity and abstraction in geometric clarity.

away from the stripped classicism of the E. Ross Adair Federal Building, in Fort Wayne, Indiana, with its hard-edged angles and hints of the old classical forms. What

James T. Foley US Post Office & Courthouse, Albany, New York, 1934, façade. Completed in 1934 by Gander & Gander, this is a superbly scaled and detailed building.

was in effect happening was a growing public awareness of the New Deal and its new style. Soon the old familiarities would be left behind for a more up-to-the-minute sensibility—smooth surfaces would become dominant over the once frenetically decorated surfaces of civic structures. Soon the rows of recognizable orders would be gone with the wind, replaced by vertical breaks in the surface plane.

The later and more sophisticated buildings from the mid-'30s and early '40s have an almost abstract quality where the general mass is expressed in a slab, the window bays assuming the role once reserved for a colonnade. The emphatic vertical expression can be relieved by a row of square windows at the top of the bay that act as a form of capital to the bay's implied column. The substitution of light and dark verticals in place of projecting piers is clear in the federal buildings in Seattle (1940), Detroit (1934), and Galveston, Texas (1937), the latter providing the most extreme example.

In all three, the façade has been treated as a plane cut by vertical shafts and framed by square and spare geometry.

The strictly ordered façade and spare interior of the US Post Office and Courthouse in Galveston, a four-square building that appears carved of a solid block of granite, was a style of civic architecture soon to be seen all over America. Inside, walls are stretched tightly over the planes and the courtroom is an example of the grid as design theme, expressed in colored woods. This visual solidity mirrored the official response to the country's financial situation, as well as defining a new aesthetic for civic buildings.

In these buildings, the architect and designer planned a cohesive design program, subtly modern and visually more compact, which emphasized the volumes and mass rather than the decoration of the building. Where there were moldings, their form was simple and direct. When called for, murals enhanced the spare walls. The total effect is one of cubic solidity.

This trend to "streamline" became more evident as the decade moved toward the '40s, and was seen in prominence at the New York World's Fair of 1939. Ultimately, this offshoot of the moderne became an American idiom well into the late '40s and early '50s. Even as the buildings became more simple, they also became more abstract. This is especially visible in the façades of the Binghamton, New York (1935), and the Los Angeles County (1938) federal buildings.

The cubic severity is softened at the James T. Foley Courthouse in Albany, New York, by the addition, at its top, of a beautiful, deeply cut wall relief. This relief serves as a form of cornice, encircling the façades and crowning the window bays with a pattern of light and shadow rendered in stone. The piers that frame the windows step back to give it a depth and modulated shading and, with its sculpted but perfectly placed décor, lend the building an almost jewel-like quality enhanced by the whiteness

James T. Foley US Post Office & Courthouse, Albany, New York, 1934, window detail.

James T. Foley US Post Office & Courthouse, Albany, New York, 1934, view showing the articulation of the window bays.

James T. Foley US Post Office & Courthouse, Albany, New York, 1934, view of entry from the interior.

Los Angeles Federal Building and Courthouse, California, 1938, main entrance. Streamlined dignity, and a wonderfully stylized ode to the classic.

of the marble. This courthouse is arguably one of the most beautiful and well proportioned of the federal buildings.Its cousin in Los Angeles takes a different route to simplicity. By its sheer verticality and size, it obviates any need for decorative elements, other than the dark green marble podium it sits upon. In many of the WPA buildings, the column or pier is used to its minimal extreme.

In the Binghamton Federal Building, the entrance is defined by the deep shadows, cast by the almost monolithic piers, without the slightest hint of décor. The entire façade is defined by sharp verticals in strict regimentation. At the Los Angeles Federal Building, six massive cylinders, with subtle fluting, present a totally convincing and powerful statement of the reductive side of the modern. They are the only decoration with any real visual weight, aside from the rigidity of the design.

The lobby of the Department of Justice Building, in Washington, DC, is a good example of the integration of the mural with the space. Here, entire walls are sheathed in buff stone reliefs set within shallow piers. The rhythm of solid wall is broken to form a screen to the stairs and the art above, where the perimeter is painted with a marvelous mural cycle. All is topped by an aluminum leafed ceiling, which crowns the room, softly reflecting light to give a serene feel. This wonderful space calls the entire era to mind, with its abstracted temple form and monumental simplicity.

By the mid-'30s, the subdued decoration that was in vogue after the Depression was being traded for an even more unadorned look. Carved and molded walls were replaced by flat undecorated planes, whose vestigial pilasters were now incised into the walls without projecting an inch.

This "invisible" classicism is clearly seen on the façade at Galveston, a federal building that truly exemplifies the "carved block of stone" look so often seen in the WPA-style public buildings. Grooves, incised in the wall piers that separate the window bays, become columns, spaced along the top of the building. Any projections from the mass of the building are hardly given emphasis at all. It is unfortunate that the window bays have been replaced by unsuitable, and badly colored, windows.

Los Angeles Federal Building and Courthouse, California, 1938, façade. A large building that due to its slender profile retains a sense of grace despite its size.

US Post Office and Courthouse, Galveston, Texas, 1937, window detail. The crisp, cut void of window bays are softened by discreet carvings in place of classic capitals.

Federal Building and US Courthouse, Peoria, Illinois, 1938, view of judicial façade. The judicial chambers are easily read on the façade, the chaste décor indicates the building's use.

Federal Building and US Courthouse, Peoria, Illinois, 1938. A rich limestone composition with beautiful bas reliefs that give emphasis to the judicial chambers with their tall window bays.

Where there was carving, it was usually a simplified bas-relief, as seen on both the Foley Courthouse and the Detroit Federal Building & US Courthouse, so subtle at times as to be almost flush with the wall. The simple carving, combined with cast or forged iron grillework, gave the unusually long façade and the main interior spaces a point of interest. Many of the buildings had separate facilities and entrances for the post office and the courthouse sections, at either end, and a long gallery was perfect for postal facilities, with plenty of natural light and circulation. The Robert A. Grant Federal Building in South Bend, Indiana, and the Federal Building and US Courthouse in Peoria, Illionois, are good examples of this long design element, though most of the civic buildings mentioned here used this form in one way or another.

The judicial chambers, usually on the upper floors, or to the side, are defined by the fenestration and, at times, through decorative carved panels around or below the windows, as in the Peoria building.

Whether the columns were fluted or left plain, with classical base and capital reduced to simple bands, the modernism of the times was on constant display. If we look at the main entrance and plaza of the 1938 Los Angeles Federal Building and Courthouse, we can see the kind of strength communicated from just a row of essentially fluted cylinders, powerfully proportioned, that stand in for the classic column. The rhythm and scale of what might be an actual colonnade or a subtle shift in the wall plane distinguishes almost all of the civic buildings of the WPA.

What sets many of these WPA-styled federal buildings apart is the handling of the volume and the spacing of the façade. Dark verticals seem carved from a light matrix, and often a border of square openings finish the vertical thrust and stand in for capitals to the implied columns. We can see this formula in Detroit, the federal building's minimal façade enlivened by a carved figurative frieze running midway around the building, activating the suavely formal design.

In a building like that of the Justice Department, the volume can be suavely elegant and ornamental, without apology. This was the showplace for the Justice Department and the usual restraint was slightly abandoned in favor of a more rich effect.

Mass, not massiveness, was the intent of the architect, and in this treatment of the vertical slab form, the building was given a modernist and at times almost playful treatment. The New Deal architecture sought an ordered design, imposing but still inviting. When used in the tower or high-rise, as in the Saint Paul City Hall, or Nebraska state capitol, there is always the emphasis on the measured space of the façade, which delineates the spatial hierarchy. This convention is readily seen in any number of civic structures where the interior space is clearly articulated, usually by the row of double-height windows, or the shadowed giant piers, as in the Binghamton or Minneapolis court buildings. In both, the emphatic expression of the vertical makes for a style unto itself—perpendicular federalism.

By 1936, exterior design and interior public space were moving toward the cubic, with much less of the high-style geometry of the previous decade, although there were still buildings that had the exuberance and whimsy of the previous generation of buildings. This reticence was in part a reaction to the Great Depression and the financial woes it engendered. Marble and bronze were still used, though a bit more sparingly, as the style assumed a boxier, austere, more ascetic feel, seen in many federal buildings that still exist today. The façade of the Binghamton Federal Building and US Courthouse, for example, is an exercise in minimal geometry.

This severity could, as at the Davidson County Courthouse in Nashville, Tennessee, become almost memorial in feeling but what usually makes the New Deal civic building particular is its visual accessibility. It both invites and gently awes at the same time.

One never feels overwhelmed in these buildings. The detail and scale, no matter how large, keep the WPA buildings within the world of the people for whom they were intended. Some are almost fortress-like in their solid mass, and yet their formidable stance can seem compelling through the placement and decoration of the entrance.

In the final analysis, most of these federal buildings are examples of different dialects of the same vernacular. Either long and low or compact and tall, the dual styles were used throughout the WPA period, both easily distinguishing themselves from the older civic buildings in their cities or towns.

Joel W. Solomon Federal Courthouse, Chattanooga, Tennessee, 1933, main façade. Monumental simplicity and clear articulation of form.

Joel W. Solomon Federal Courthouse, Chattanooga, Tennessee, 1933, corner detail.

Certainly one of the most beautiful and successful of the long and low design articulation is another Tennessee federal building; the Joel W. Solomon Courthouse of 1933, in Chattanooga, perfectly exemplifies the period and the style. In its massing and restrained decoration, it dominates its site with a powerful yet graceful presence. The courthouse was recognized in 1938 by the American Institute of Architects as one of the 150 best buildings that had been constructed since 1918, and it exemplifies everything that we think of when federal moderne is brought to mind. The five-sto-

Joel W. Solomon Federal Courthouse, Chattanooga, Tennessee, 1933, postal lobby. Pale yellow and green marble make for an arresting interior. The terrazzo floor with its chevron pattern gives a sense of motion to the more static vertical and horizontal rhythm of the walls.

Joel W. Solomon Federal Courthouse, Chattanooga, Tennessee, 1933, detail of wall. This detail shows the articulation of pilaster and plane with its decorative bronze grillework.

Joel W. Solomon Federal Courthouse, Chattanooga, Tennessee, 1933, main lobby. As beautiful a space indoors as out, the entrance lobby is paneled in luxurious marbles and features pendant lighting.

ry building, clad in white marble, clearly states its civic purpose in detail, including the huge carved eagles at its corners that seem to grow out of the marble itself. The building is of the dual pavilion type, joined by a long, low, and drawn-out central portion that visually explains the purpose of the space. The entrance pavilions, approached by wide sets of steps flanked by the geometric eagles, add to the formal and quietly imposing feel.

Inside, the mood is decidedly more exuberant though still restrained. The yellow and black marble walls and terrazzo flooring set in chevron patterns set a lively and geometric cadence. The original bronze and aluminum grilles are in place and intact allowing one to sense the space in its original vision. Inside the lobby spaces, the lighting fixtures have a clear art deco look but still fall inside the federal moderne canon of subdued formality. Each corresponding entrance pavilion contains a softly curving stair of black marble with simple geometric motifs in cast aluminum. These lobbies are separated from the main postal floor by screens of fluted black marble piers that, with the original lighting and the yellow sienna marble walls, create a noble portal to the ether of the building's functions.

The attention to detail, usually high in these buildings, is even more pronounced. The highly considered way the cast aluminum postal screens are set and spaced in the sienna marble walls creates a composition framed by the black marble pilasters. The lighting, indirect and concealed in an aluminum trough that runs the length of the hall, casts a glow over the curved ceiling. The entire space and the attendant courtroom are complete orchestrations of a more sophisticated use of the federal moderne than found in most public space of its era.

These dialects, used consistently throughout the era, became symbolic of the federal moderne style of American deco architecture. While some are more complex and stylish or more horizontal in appearance, all are muscular buildings, both inside and out, with measured white marble façades and often the original black and yellow sienna marble interiors. The Davidson County Courthouse in Nashville,

Joel W. Solomon Federal Courthouse, Chattanooga, Tennessee, 1933, stair rail detail.

Courthouse (Metropolitan Courthouse), Nashville, Tennessee, 1936, façade. Stolid and solid with more than a hint of the classic, the building stands strong and four-square.

Tennessee, "heavier" in presence, recalls the Doric order of the Lincoln Memorial, but with a streamlined sensibility. Its lobby is a harmonious blend of green marble and terrazzo with four murals representing the seasons framed between the double-height piers that are capped with streamlined ionic order capitols. The lobby space is expansive and well coordinated in its harmonious decorative elements.

The essential design element that one is most aware of when seeing these buildings of the '30s is their solidity. As in all of the WPA-style buildings, what is important are clean lines and stolid mass, whether in a modest post office or a huge federal office.

Davidson County Courthouse (Metropolitan Courthouse), Nashville, Tennessee, 1936, sculpture. Creating an almost gothic sensibility, the main portals are framed by three-dimensional wall reliefs.

Davidson County Courthouse (Metropolitan Courthouse), Nashville, Tennessee, 1936, murals in lobby. A nice integration of the wall treatment with the materials of the large and lofty space.

Chapter Three: Form and Function
Details of the Design

Federal Building and US Courthouse, Binghamton, New York, 1935, façade. Another use of the colonnade, this time reduced to the almost abstract form and so very different from the Davidson County Courthouse and its evocative colonnade.

The first and most important impression that a building presents is its face, or façade, which, along with the lobby, are what form the lasting impressions for the average citizen. The first glimpse of white marble seen on one's approach sets the stage for the civic experience that follows.

Certainly, the view should express the dignity and public utility of the structure but, as we know, FDR wanted a complete recognition of his New Deal and its zeal to come through, to help lift spirits in the financial crisis of the mid-'30s. All of the elements designated for use in these civic places were thoughtfully considered, and though there were budgetary issues, of course, the best of what could be attained within those restrictions was used.

It was imperative for the building to create a sense of pride in the local community. Marble and granite were in the forefront of cladding, both for exteriors and interiors, the latter being at times veneered in contrasting colors or patterns typical of the style. The lights and fixtures were usually custom designs or refitted to suit the needs of the designer. Whatever the case, the favored material for the interior metalwork—railings , grilles, and lighting standards—was bronze, though later in the decade much use would be made of aluminum.

The lobby with the façade—those two most important public features a visitor would experience—focused on length and/

Davidson County Courthouse (Metropolitan Courthouse), Nashville, Tennessee, 1936, entrance. Art was used extensively in and on New Deal buildings. Entrances were paid special attention, as shown with this building's main entrance, firmly cut into the base of the building and balanced by the flatness of the mosaic square above each portal.

or height. The main public spaces, as expressed on the exterior, were of a generous height, letting air and light in through the walls of windows. If the building had dual purposes, such as serving as a federal courthouse as well as a post office, the

Federal Trade Commission Building, Washington, DC, 1938, apex view. Like many of the other WPA buildings in the capital, this is a good example of the stripped classic moderne with a leaning towards the neoclassic idiom, but simplified.

judicial rooms were equally generous in scale and material and were located on the second floor.

Another design convention, favored by many architects, was more minimal and abstract, as in Binghamton, where the entrance to the judicial and postal section is expressed as an opening in the screen of monolithic columns that encircle the building.

The Binghamton Federal Building uses a central approach where the entrance portal, really a recessed portico of deeply off-set bays, is behind a continuous row of square undecorated columns. These tall piers project from the façade but remain flush within the form of the façade and encircle the building. The regimented geometry makes for a vivid show of light and shadows. As the sun passes, the form and structure shifts with the day into an abstract pattern of light and dark verticals.

One of my favorite buildings for its truly modern and novel interpolation of the federal moderne style, Binghamton's façades and interior with its wonderful mural decorations remain much as they were when new.

More compact and taller, the central portals on the Davidson County Courthouse in Nashville, Tennessee, are deeply recessed and shadowed openings that seem to be carved from the mass. Three glowing, golden mosaics are set flush above the portals, and the wonderful statues that flank the doors distinguish them as the entrance, though quietly, as right above a colonnade of sleekly modern Doric columns stand in horizontal regimen.

The device of a slight change in the height or plane for this emphasis is seen in the Sioux City Federal Building and US Courthouse and Hartford's Cotter Federal Building, where giant streamlined columns frame the entrance bays, leaving no doubt to their importance—not to mention the giant eagles perched ominously above. Earlier, more tentative attempts were often more rigid in their mass and detail.

In Albany's James T. Foley US Post Office and Courthouse, we find the perfect synthesis of mass and class with a more integrated block than most in its balance of solid and void and its wonderful ability to look lighter than its mass belies. Sensitively handled and elegant, it is an exemplary picture of the federal moderne. As in many of the other federal buildings, a lateral façade holds the courthouse or the post office and is expressed in a series of tall bays and alternating, simply defined piers that step back in increments to soften the presence of the pier. The beautiful-

Old Social Security Building, Washington, DC, 1935, corner view. A relatively unadorned building, save for its interior murals, it is able to convey the idea of grandeur, though minimal, in its freestanding screen of piers.

Federal Building and US Courthouse, Binghamton, New York, 1935, main entrance. This type of monolithic rhythm in light and dark is reminiscent of many buildings of the period; this particular building in Binghamton has an almost fascist sensibility.

Robert N. C. Nix, Sr. Federal Building and US Courthouse, Philadelphia, Pennsylvania, 1937, bas-relief entrance. Figures of stylized civic aspirations flank the main entrance to this beautiful building.

Federal Building and US Courthouse, Peoria, Illinois, 1938, carved figures.

ly integrated and carved frieze above the window bays serves as an extended capital.

Sculpted bas-relief was often used to emphasize the entrance or other important architectural features. One such relief frames the entrance at the Nix Federal Courthouse in Philadelphia. Less subtle but very effective are the almost freestanding figures in Peoria. The entire court façade is delineated by them, set in panels beneath the tall courtroom windows.

An interesting outgrowth was a modified, tower-like central bay as in the federal building in Sioux City, Iowa. Here, shallow detailing enhances the planer qualities of the new design. Inside the building is a well-ordered version of the stripped classic federal moderne, the stairway being an enthusiastic nod to the art of the metalworker as it flows in a golden hued bronze to a baroquely shaped and fluted newel. Throughout the building are numerous decorative devices set into the simple walls that give a golden and light touch to the beautifully proportioned spaces lit by hang-

E. Ross Adair Federal Building & US Courthouse, Fort Wayne, Indiana, 1932, façade.
A simple and somewhat rigidly elegant stone structure, clearly articulated and with simply stated authority.

ing pendant fixtures from a simple, geometrically gilded ceiling.

The foyer and hall of the Cotter building in Hartford use particularly interesting hanging pendants that are set in recessed and painted panels down the length of the double-height room, adding visual interest

to the long and quiet space. This standard formula of double-height foyer with a central pendant hung from the ceiling and marble walls in contrasting colors was used throughout the era. The lighting, aside from these pendants, is usually either indirect up-lighting or, in the unique case of the

E. Ross Adair Federal Building & US Courthouse, Fort Wayne, Indiana, 1932, main hall. Little hoopla. Lots of marble in light tones adds visual interest to the stoic space.

E. Ross Adair Federal Building & US Courthouse, Fort Wayne, Indiana, 1932, window detail. Simple elegant details and the rich use of marble give the space its sense of importance.

Davidson County Courthouse (Metropolitan Courthouse), Nashville, Tennessee, 1936, detail of square column in lobby.

Davidson County Courthouse (Metropolitan Courthouse), Nashville, Tennessee, 1936, mosaic over entrance.

Davidson County Courthouse (Metropolitan Courthouse), Nashville, Tennessee, 1936, terrazzo flooring design. A typical terrazzo design with slightly Grecian overtones is in keeping with the building's stripped classic design.

Davidson County Courthouse (Metropolitan Courthouse), Nashville, Tennessee, 1936, staircase.

Kansas City City Hall, Kansas City, Missouri, 1937, view of paneling in courtroom. Wood in all its varieties was used in intricate veneers in many court chambers.

Minneapolis post office, a fantastically long light trough in bronze that runs directly down the center of the post office, indirectly illuminating the long hall.

This novel design feature was most effective in illuminating the long and lofty room that usually housed the post office. Outside, the dual purposes of postal and judicial services could be visually addressed with this articulation, almost standard for much of the era.

The Peoria, Illinois, Federal Building's lateral space is clad in creamy pink and cream marble and terrazzo set in patterned style and richly ornamented by the original metalwork that frames the postal windows. Above the tall window bays are octagonal gilded plaques that add a note of smartness to the impressively lofty space.

Inside Nashville's Davidson County Courthouse, the space is quite specific and grand. It is a large double-height interior with a set of murals depicting the seasons and framed by a simplified Ionic order with cleverly stylized capitals. The walls are of highly veined marble, and the floors are patterned terrazzo that echoes the ornamental capitals.

Like much civic space produced during the decade, the effect is stylish without being flashy. The rooms are well removed from the everyday world, with a feeling of calm security.

Unlike their European counterparts, these interior spaces are impressive but never bombastic. As part of the federal program they were designed to be user-friendly and remain so today. The "whole" of the building creates a consistent aesthetic ensemble, instead of having separate rooms and their own unique lighting fixtures and grilles. Every design element is interrelated.

In all of the public space, one thing was consistent: the use of marble. Entire rooms were sheathed in polished stone, while precious or fine local woods were reserved for the judicial sections of the buildings to help acoustics, and to create an effect of sobriety. These lofty and spacious courtrooms are refined and exude a sense of jurisprudence.

At times, as in Austin's US Courthouse or the Peoria Federal Building and US Courthouse, interior paneling assumes a graphic quality that echoes the building. For the most part, though, court space was kept minimally decorative with allusions to the federal eagle and subtle moldings and grillework set in highly grained and polished walls.

Federal Building and US Courthouse, Binghamton, New York, 1935, mural.

At New York's Binghamton Federal Building and US Courthouse the mural decoration works in harmony with the architecture. The consistency of materials makes this lobby spacious and rich, as the paintings adapt to the wall treatments. The same use of the mural as a visual relief and colorful addition are found in the lobbies of the Department of the Interior and the Department of Justice Building. In both, the color and meaning of the imagery add a note of humanity to the massive formal plans.

Lighting was a major design feature and used not only to illuminate the workspace but also as a decorative concept. Sources

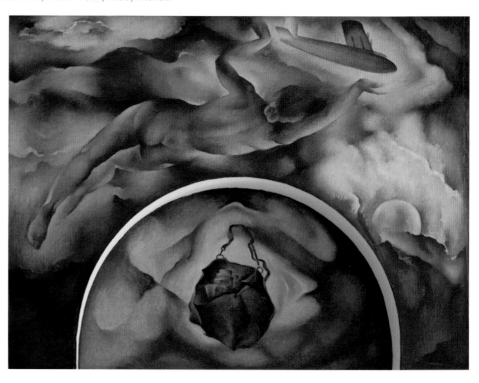

Federal Building and US Courthouse, Binghamton, New York, 1935, mural.

US Post Office, Courthouse, and Custom House, Key West, Florida, 1933, entrance torchères. Typical of the type of lighting standard found on many WPA buildings.

of artificial illumination were not confined to sconces and chandeliers but were also hidden in light troughs and decorative moldings.

Bronze urns could be fitted with up-lighting to cast an indirect glow over entire rooms, with light reflected off painted or decorated ceilings. Concealed and indirect illumination had just become popular and was used for its greatest effect in large public spaces, the US Post Office in Minneapolis, Minnesota, having one of the largest single fixtures of this type, a bronze chandelier stretching across the lobby at a length of about 350 feet. Missouri's Kansas City municipal building and Albany's Foley Courthouse show the use of up-lights well. The fifth-floor lobby to the Law Library of the Justice Department is an excellent example of indirect and reflected light.

Classic torchères are also used to great effect in many buildings inside and out.

Department of Interior, Washington, DC, 1941, murals in hall.

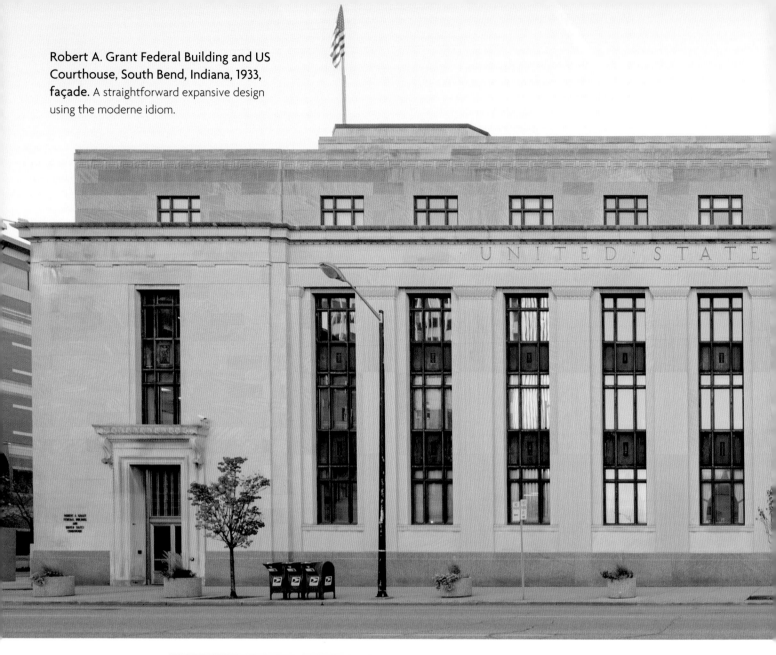

Robert A. Grant Federal Building and US Courthouse, South Bend, Indiana, 1933, façade. A straightforward expansive design using the moderne idiom.

Robert A. Grant Federal Building and US Courthouse, South Bend, Indiana, 1933, view of lobby.

These lighting standards, usually at the building's entrance, set a tone of expectation as well as welcome. Standard stanchions were typically used to emphasize the entry or some part of the lobby that needed the symbolism. New Deal federal building space usually involved a foyer and lobby laid out according to a standard plan. A long post office section usually occupied the central portion of the building and could be readily located on the outside by the large windows that provided light and air. Where there was a federal court or offices, a second lobby could be found at the opposite end; it connected with the post office space, as well. As noted, while economic times were tough, the use of marble and metal is often extravagant, if simply designed, and at times the color and juxtaposition of the materials add a

fanciful note to the interiors, as in the John W. McCormack Post Office and Courthouse in Boston or the United States Custom House in Philadelphia. This style in latter years, for lack of a proper name, became known in the vernacular as "post office style" and was primarily used when describing the painted decoration, as the building's style had no real name.

For most Americans living away from the coastal urban centers, these post offices were the first modern buildings they would see.

"Post" modern in the truest sense, these buildings were examples of the "new" for many who had never before been in anything more modern than a filling station or movie theater.

Robert A. Grant Federal Building and US Courthouse, South Bend, Indiana, 1933, window detail.

Chapter Four: Simply Moderne
Modernism with an American Twist

St. Paul City Hall and Ramsey County Courthouse, Saint Paul, Minnesota, 1932. The quintessential in moderne civic tower buildings—coolly elegant.

CITY HALL & COURT HOUSE

For the average American in the '30s, exposure to modern architecture was generally limited to visits to department stores or, more frequently, large movie palaces, where skyscrapers were featured in many movies. The few civic structures built as "towers," such as the Saint Paul City Hall or the even more energetic Kansas City City Hall show a bit of the West Coast theatrical style. This form of the idealized modern tower, created on a vastly smaller scale than buildings in New York City or Chicago, was nonetheless a familiar idiom to the public, who had seen its progenitors on the silver screen. Once accepted on the screen, the foreign element of the modern—read French—was more readily digested and assimilated into daily American life.

St. Paul City Hall and Ramsey County Courthouse, Saint Paul, Minnesota, 1932, lobby entrance. About as art deco you will get in a federal public building, this building is cinematic in its scale and visual splendor.

Kansas City City Hall, Kansas City, Missouri, 1937, tower. A small skyscraper, at home in any city.

Kansas City Hall, Kansas City, Missouri, 1937, lobby chandelier and stairs to mezzanine.

Kansas City City Hall, Kansas City, Missouri, 1937, view of lobby with indirect lighting.

Municipal Auditorium, Kansas City, Missouri, 1934, view of lobby. A dynamic use of the fluorescent lighting, popular at the time. A very suitable design for the shape and scale of the space, the lobby gives a nice prelude to the auditorium.

The City Hall in Kansas City is a tower in the moderne style, though not quite as emphatic as Saint Paul's. Its lobby's use of rich materials such as the bronze elevator doors in the art deco federal motif and the reference to the grand lobby space of the mega theater give a familiar touch to the otherwise coolly impressive space. Kansas City was quite at home with the new style and in its municipal auditorium, we see the most moderne of any large assembly space built during the era.

The public's growing familiarity with the details and materials of these buildings

Kansas City Municipal Auditorium, 1934, theater. A very successful expression of modernist space, reminiscent of the now demolished Center Theatre at Rockefeller Center.

Municipal Auditorium, Kansas City, Missouri, 1934, view of convention hall. A big, contemporary space for the masses to enjoy sports events and gatherings. The ceiling is particularly attractive.

also helped them accept the style as it spread to other forms of art and architecture.

International expositions and fairs, as well as cinemas, both so popular during this period, helped disseminate the visual ideas of modernity to the public. Of particular interest was the Century of Progress Exposition of 1933–34 in Chicago that set the stage for the complete acceptance of the new look in architecture and interior design in America.

This new style was, in its beginnings, meant for the sophisticated and urbane but in time would be adapted to mass

Approach to Croton Reservoir Bridge, Westchester County, New York, 1931. There were very few places the New Deal did not leave some of the new style.

Parkway stanchion, 1930s. Even the most utilitarian objects were given attention.

consumption and altered to fit almost any discipline. It was even used for decorative effect on the highways and bridges that were being built across the country.

The Croton Reservoir bridge in New York State is a good example of the design elements of pier and recess being altered to form a formal approach to the span.

The style even made appearances at seaside recreational spaces, themselves a style unto their own. Jones Beach is arguably the finest of the public bathing facilities made possible through the WPA with help from Robert Moses. The wonderful beach is still a popular destination. Less well known but no less well planned is Jacob Reis Park beach in Queens, New York, with its expansive pavilion and bathhouses and the iconic twin beacons that have welcomed visitors since its streamlined esplanade and restaurant were opened in 1932.

Jacob Riis Park, Queens, Long Island, 1932–33, bathhouse and pavilion. Moderne for the masses—the queens Riviera.

Reis Park was accessible from the city by car, on the new WPA-created parkways, as well as by public transportation. The oceanfront restaurant pavilion and bathhouses were thoughtfully designed with flair. The main bath and food concession is a classic example of this trend to the moderne with its curving walls of glass block and tapering spires; it figuratively shouts that it is there for fun and forever. The row of squat massive cylinders that form the boardwalk colonnade help to

Jacob Riis Park, Queens, Long Island, 1932–33, esplanade and columns. A real sense of style was attempted here to help the masses achieve their own seaside fantasies of the casinos and clubs of the rich.

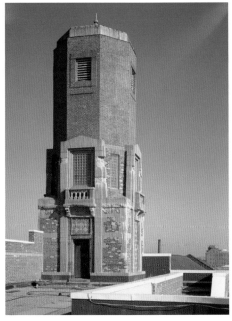

Jacob Riis Park, Queens, Long Island, 1932–33, light tower. The twin focal points of the main bathhouse have an art deco look.

Aquatic Park Maritime Museum (Bathhouse Building), San Francisco, 1939, general view. A bit of Hollywood on San Francisco Bay.

Aquatic Park Maritime Museum (Bathhouse Building), San Francisco, 1939, entrance.

Aquatic Park Maritime Museum (Bathhouse Building), San Francisco, 1939, **general view.** Like some big white ocean liner at quayside, the building seems to be about to depart.

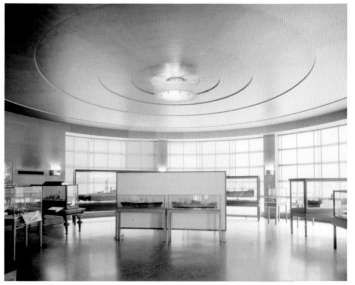

Aquatic Park Maritime Museum (Bathhouse Building), San Francisco, 1939, **interior.** No set designer in the movies could do better to give off a sense of being at sea on a great liner.

enforce its stance against time and tide. All of the design conventions of the '30s were used to their most festive effect.

Its curving walls and nautical feel remind

one of the similarly streamlined Aquatic Park and Bathhouse, built in 1939 as a joint project of the WPA and the City of San Francisco.

Here, one feels truly on a ship at sea. The streamlined curves and walls of glass are used to nautical effect; the feeling is like being on a great ocean liner. All form

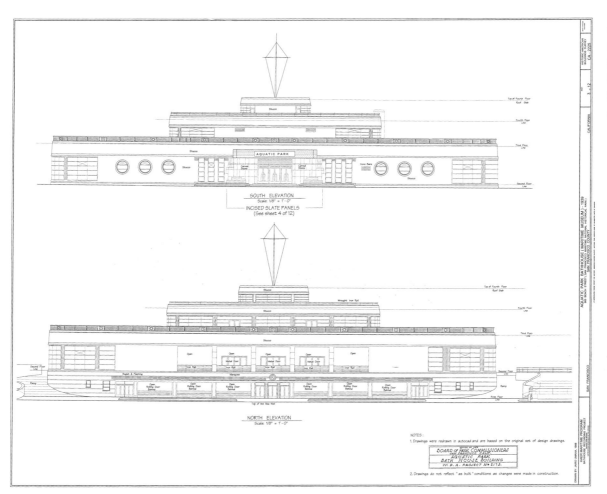

Aquatic Park Maritime Museum (Bathhouse Building), San Francisco, 1939, elevations.

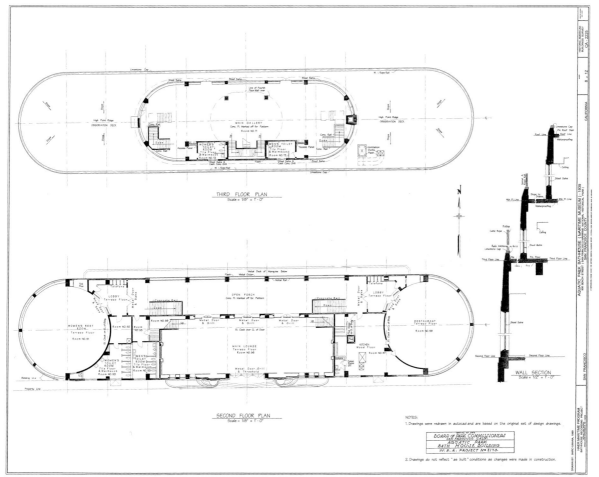

Aquatic Park Maritime Museum (Bathhouse Building), San Francisco, 1939, plans.

and decoration are taken from the sea and ships.

The lobby transforms into an underwater grotto with highly colored and leafed murals of a fantastical underwater scene. Upstairs, one could be on the veranda of the SS *Normandie* or *Queen Mary* at sea. This extreme of streamlining was not nearly as common within the government agencies and was more adapted to commercial usage such as theaters or amusement establishments. Perhaps it was just too forward and radical for the more majestically minded bureaucracy.

The art and mosaics that cover the porch facing the sea have, again, nautical motifs—turtles, sailboats, fish—all rendered in white and green highly glazed tiles. The subject is apropos of the site and a delight to view as one walks the esplanade facing the bay. The art is very abstract, as is the entire form of the building and particularly its entrance. With shallow lines incised into the dark green slate surround of the building's entry, the abstract world of undersea motifs was created by the artist Sargent Johnson and contrasts wonderfully with the stark white of the superstructure. The buildings modernity and novelty were well received, and it is still maintained and used intact.

The building has been critically acclaimed for the freshness of the art and architecture and its "fun" aspect, appropriate to building's use.

The interior is decorated with a cycle of murals depicting an undersea world in silvers and blues by Sargent, who was one of the only two black artists in the California WPA program and a well-known and respected figure in the art world. His work blends perfectly with the sleekness of the building and unites the machine age and nautical forms in an appealing construct. In fact, the new design quotient was firmly instilled in the public eye by the mid-'30s, and by the '40s, the style was ubiquitous across the land.

The New York World's Fair of 1939, on the eve of the coming war, was the last

Aquatic Park Maritime Museum (Bathhouse Building), San Francisco, 1939, view of murals in lobby.

cohesive example of this streamlined federal moderne all in one set place. The pavilions and exhibits were streamlined and simply detailed. The walls and general décor were spare in contrast to the Century of Progress six years earlier, where the style was first Americanized.

Time had changed the exuberance of design to a wartime solidarity, and in its last gasp the civic program of FDR and the WPA chose a refined modernity that we still think of in our collective memory of what modern was.

Chapter Five: Paul Cret's Influence
Developing a Recognizable Signature

Federal Reserve Building (Marriner S. Eccles Building), Washington, DC, 1937. Designed by Paul Cret, one of the best known of the architects for the WPA.

The interwar years played host to various threads of modernism through the many completions of new buildings by many architects, most of whom had made their reputations in the civic and public domain. The most exemplary of the style was Paul Cret, pronounced "cray," whose signature building, the new Federal Reserve in Washington, DC, was to be a centerpiece in the development of the Federal Triangle, a 70-acre site between the White House and the Capitol, and play a large role in the stylistic progression of the New Deal buildings.

Cret's influence on the architecture of the WPA and PWA cannot be overestimated, and the Federal Reserve Building is a seminal building as far as federal moderne style is concerned.

The construction of the Federal Reserve Building is perhaps one of the most important moments in the building program of the New Deal. The Federal Reserve, itself an outcome of the Great Depression, was created to build confidence in the ravaged banking structure. Its public home in Washington, DC, was to be the outward symbol of that confidence in marble and bronze.

Cret was classically trained in the beaux arts style and this is clear in the formal approach to the building. In all of his civic work, one can see the subtle classicism reduced to the most common decorative denominator.

The interior spaces of Cret's buildings are spare yet elegant due to the richness of the material and their proportions, which stem from his beaux arts training. At the Fed, as with many of the more important of these buildings, architectural treatment

Federal Reserve Building (Marriner S. Eccles Building), Washington, DC, 1937, drawing of stair hall. The space, created for the real pocketbook of the nation, has a feel of complete poise. Like some Greco-Roman vault, the space exudes confidence.

Department of Interior, Washington, DC, 1936, stair mural decoration. Art is found throughout the building as befitting the creative side of the PWA.

is formal. The progression goes from a large steeped terrace to the grand stair to the entrance portico. This is not a freestanding set of columns but four massive piers of white marble that emerge from the surface of the façade and project outwards.

These piers became a model for many of the succeeding civic structures during the period. The entering visitor immediately becomes aware of the atrium that Cret so cleverly placed at the heart of the building. The severity of the stone material against the richness of wrought iron and rather light Doric columns creates a tension with the planar insistence of unadorned walls. The beauty of Cret's and many of his contemporaries' work lies in this ability to adopt the conservative and neoclassic style to the modern, which was to become, of course, one of the defining factors of the

classic moderne of the '30s and '40s.

In a country whose banks just went bankrupt, the restraint and sobriety that Cret gave the space is reassuring. The Fed's two building lobbies, one in Washington, DC, and one in Philadelphia, are both by Cret and are extremely chaste and understated. One can imagine these grand but spare interiors had the program allowed the sort of colorful murals that are found in the Department of the Interior Building. These paintings enliven and relieve the insistent orthogonal of the central hall while expanding the space around the grand stair.

It is hard to make the connection between Cret's work in Philadelphia and the Cincinnati Union Terminal complex, for which he helped design the interior rotunda. Though not specifically a project of the

WPA, Union Terminal is a product of the times and Depression-minded America but is out of sync with the more boxy feel of its cohorts. It does, however, in the most unexpected and wonderful way, express the mass and solidity of the form in a huge arching wall of vertical elements that are anything but frivolous.

Its grand arc of glass and vertical piers is light-years away from the previously popular classical arch or the contemporaneous boxy marble moderne.

The interior, all radial arches and layered ceiling, recalls Radio City Music Hall. The successive half-circular arcs that telescope and indirectly light the rotunda display a different side of the architect. These arcs and half-circles, combined with the ever-present stepped and tapering pier, were used throughout the structure to great

Union Terminal, Cincinnati, Ohio, 1933, interior view of grand arch. The Radio City of civic buildings—a visual performance in stone.

effect both on the exterior and as the entrance approach that runs through and inside the perimeter walls. The approach in Cincinnati's Union Terminal is a destination in itself made of a series of rising geometric pools that echoes and reflects the massive station. This desire to blend the principles of the beaux arts with the modern was used by almost every architect and designer working for the New Deal.

The sweeping curves and colorful interior show another side of the architect who could design as severe and classic moderne a civic structure as the Philadelphia Federal Reserve. With its cool interior space and simplified form, it stands at the oppo-

Union Terminal, Cincinnati, Ohio, 1933, exterior and approach. Though not strictly a WPA building, the terminal is typical of public and many of the more exuberant civic structures of the decade.

Union Terminal, Cincinnati, Ohio, interior. The terminal's designer, Paul Cret, later designed the Federal Reserve building in DC, where the quintessence of reserve was never more adventuresome.

Union Terminal, Cincinnati, Ohio, 1933, interior.

Federal Reserve Building, Philadelphia, Pennsylvania, 1932, detail.

site pole of the design spectrum from Cincinnati. Instead of the colorful murals and circular theme are measured piers and columns of dark marble visually supporting the white arc (the ceiling) with the federal eagle that immediately identifies the space as important. The building is large, but the architect skillfully handled its height by running a subtle cornice around its mid-point, and reduced all of the stonework and carving to simple forms.

The imposing walls are more scaled to the street, as it sits in Center City, Philadelphia, and is part of the civic scene.

Another of Cret's successful New Deal buildings, and a fully realized example of federal moderne at its most elegantly classical, is the Eldon B. Mahon US Courthouse and former post office in Fort Worth, Texas, built in 1934. Like all of Cret's work, the building is spare and sensitively proportioned, using the finest of materials, especially in the court chambers on the upper floors. This building is an icon of the American art deco style at its most refined. The original three main entrance doors of bronze and glass are defined by a set of four tall aluminum and glass light standards that accentuate the modernity and light the pueblo deco grillework and low relief that adorns the entrance and the window trims of the entire building. The original postal lobby is intact with its marble walls and patterned terrazzo floor; combined with the geometric dome, this is the art deco federal style at its most luxe.

The courtrooms are especially notable for their clean design as well as the superb and high quality of the materials, including rare and precious woods and marble. The

Union Terminal, Cincinnati, Ohio, 1933.

Union Terminal, Cincinnati, Ohio, 1933, interior motor entry.

Federal Reserve Building, Philadelphia, Pennsylvania, 1932, exterior. Paul Cret at his most stoic and severe; a fortress-like structure for money.

Federal Reserve Building, Philadelphia, Pennsylvania, 1932, interior entry.

Federal Reserve Building, Philadelphia, Pennsylvania, 1932, interior main hall. Rich materials with simple but elegant details and proportions.

Court of Appeals is especially striking with twenty-two-foot-high walls of oak and columns of yellow marble all culminating in the three oil-on-canvas panels by Frank Mechau, commissioned in 1938 under the PWA's art programs and installed in 1940. It is especially nice how the soft arc of the wall on which the art is mounted and the curved corners of the room create a strongly streamlined effect. (See image on page 19 in chapter one.)

A large building, its size is mitigated by the way the window bays, as in the Foley Courthouse in Albany, have been treated as a series of softly stepped verticals with low relief and projecting spandrels.

Eldon B. Mahon Federal Courthouse, Fort Worth, Texas, 1934, façade. The spare design by Paul Cret and Wiley Clarkson, a Texan, is elegantly civic chic.

Eldon B. Mahon Federal Courthouse, Fort Worth, Texas, 1934, main façade. Thoughtfully considered and proportioned, the building's details and decoration are of the highest standard.

Eldon B. Mahon Federal Courthouse, Fort Worth, Texas, 1934, detail.

Eldon B. Mahon Federal Courthouse, Fort Worth, Texas, 1934, entrance to court.

Eldon B. Mahon Federal Courthouse, Fort Worth, Texas, 1934, main courtroom. Restrained art deco—the room is grand but comfortable in its materials.

Eldon B. Mahon Federal Courthouse, Fort Worth, Texas, 1934, ceiling of lobby.

Eldon B. Mahon Federal Courthouse, Fort Worth, Texas, 1934, stair detail.

Chapter Six: From Sea to Shining Sea
A Lasting and Widespread Impression

Old Department of War Building (now State Department Building), a.k.a. Harry S. Truman Federal Building, Washington, DC, 1941, lobby.

Old Department of War Building (now State Department Building), a.k.a. Harry S. Truman Federal Building, Washington, DC, 1941. This very authoritative building comes close to the architecture of the Italian Regime under Mussolini. An almost psychedelic war mural is in its otherwise bland lobby.

One thing that most, if not all, of the WPA buildings I chose for this book place an emphasis on is "weight," or visual mass, and most show an almost sculptural, though not plastic, use of form where the solid basic rectilinear shape is cut and set back to make for visual plays of light and dark. The effect was by no means accidental. The New Deal desired to instill the idea of stability in communities, and architecture became the perfect symbol of that stability. This movement in design in the United States was taking place at the same time as nationalistic spirits grew in Germany and Italy; in these countries the return to order became a harbinger of the total state control of the fascists. Theirs was an either more cerebral or more dour form of modernism. Here in America, we wanted the buildings to talk, but in a familiar and upbeat tone, not in the bombastic shouts of Munich or Berlin.

While most WPA buildings did follow a common federal moderne template, there are some that came close to the modern

Old Department of War Building (now State Department Building), a.k.a. Harry S. Truman Federal Building, Washington, DC, 1941, mural.

designs of the European school. The old Department of War building is one of these.

The original portion of the Harry S. Truman Federal Building, formerly known as the War Department building, is a well-executed example of the strict classical style with modernist elements. The design is spartan and minimal but in the lobby is an explosion of color in Kindred McLeary's 1942 *Defense of Human Freedoms* mural, which clearly expresses the purpose of this building!

The Library of Virginia in Richmond had its third home, from 1940 to 1997, in a building on Capitol Street. Now known as the Patrick Henry Building, it was previously known as the Old State Library or the Virginia State Library and Archives and Virginia Supreme Court. The building presents a formidable exterior bare of all extraneous décor as well as sleek and minimally decorated interiors. I am sure mural decoration was at some point planned for the vast expanses of plain wall in the reading room, but the stylish wood veneers that curve around columns and walls in the lobby are smart and light.

With its imposingly solid walls that create deep patterns of shadow and windows that seem to be carved from the solid mass, the Richmond building is an especially fine example of moving to the abstracted and modern. The few decorative elements at its entrance make for a formidable building. The interior space with its tall attenuated columns is quietly impressive. The abbre-

Virginia State Library Building and Courthouse, a.k.a. Patrick Henry Building, Richmond, Virginia, 1938, exterior view. This truly monumental and stolid building seems carved of a solid block of granite. The windows are almost cut into the solid and make for deep light and dark contrasts.

viated façades and the careful placement of windows would lead to an even more abstract form.

The Nix Federal Courthouse of 1937 is a fine example of this more modern civic understatement. It is a big building but its skillful massing and use of decorative detail make a particularly fine expression of the more reductive form of the style. The spandrels, usually a place for carving, are reduced to three horizontal lightly convex bands that quietly emphasize the window bays. The large lobby with its indirect lighting and sculpted marble frieze above the elevator bank is impressive in its reticence.

The novel use of lighting deeply recessed in circular depressions in the ceiling give the interior a futuristic look. The twin carved bas-reliefs at the entrance give a

Virginia State Library Building and Courthouse, a.k.a. Patrick Henry Building, Richmond, Virginia, 1938, interior. As spartan as the exterior, the interior is sleekly modern and spacious.

Virginia State Library Building and Courthouse, a.k.a. Patrick Henry Building, Richmond, Virginia, 1938, interior.

Robert N. C. Nix, Sr. Federal Building and US Courthouse, Philadelphia, Pennsylvania, 1937. Stepped back from its granite base, the building rises five more stories, a penthouse adding interest to the façade.

Robert N. C. Nix, Sr. Federal Building and US Courthouse, Philadelphia, Pennsylvania, 1937. Restrained modernism, with smooth transitions of form.

Robert N. C. Nix, Sr. Federal Building and US Courthouse, Philadelphia, Pennsylvania, 1937. Decorative carvings above the elevator bank. The interior features rich materials and subtle colors.

Robert N. C. Nix, Sr. Federal Building and US Courthouse, Philadelphia, Pennsylvania, 1937. Window spandrel showing the simple decorative element defining the floors.

Robert N. C. Nix, Sr. Federal Building and US Courthouse, Philadelphia, Pennsylvania, 1937, bas-relief.

human touch to the large but well-proportioned building.

As the new decade and the winds of war approached, the more simple façade became the norm. You see this in the Detroit and Seattle federal buildings built just as the '40s began to unravel. In the years leading up to the war and after, the style reflected the mood of world affairs. The rare marble and refined space became less important than the function. In these latter buildings, the grand foyer and lobby spaces were not generally as lofty as those of their earlier counterparts. With the Detroit and Seattle buildings, the reductive classic phase of the later federal moderne becomes more the vogue. Both are ordered civic spaces with their emphasis on spare but noble proportion.

An interesting holdout to the grand experience was the John Adams Building, an addition to the Library of Congress built just before the war in 1939. It is a genuinely four-square and simply defined building with a series of geometric solids laid one upon the other in a cubic stack. The only real exterior decorations are the huge doors that are detailed in the best WPA manner of solidity (the original bronze doors were recently replaced with kiln-cast glass cre-

Robert N. C. Nix, Sr. Federal Building and US Courthouse, Philadelphia, Pennsylvania, 1937, clock. Streamlined modernity in the lobby, where even the clock reflects the more sober aesthetic of the late '30s and early '40s.

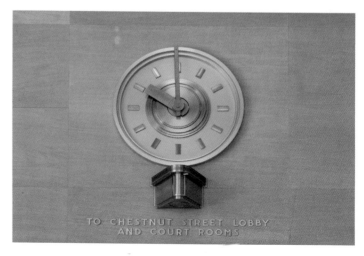

Robert N. C. Nix, Sr. Federal Building and US Courthouse, Philadelphia, Pennsylvania, 1937.

Robert N. C. Nix, Sr. Federal Building and US Courthouse, Philadelphia, Pennsylvania, 1937, hall.

John Adams Building, Library of Congress, Washington, DC, 1939, façade. A simple, stripped classical structure of white marble with a subtle art deco influence.

John Adams Building, Library of Congress, Washington, DC, 1939, reading room. The somewhat sober reading room with the Ezra Winter mural, a conservative painting but a wall of needed color in the vast space.

John Adams Building, Library of Congress, Washington, DC, 1939, elevator door.

John Adams Building, Library of Congress, Washington, DC, 1939, owl motif.

John Adams Building, Library of Congress, Washington, DC, 1939, wall detail.

War Memorial Building, Jackson, Mississippi, 1939, façade. A small ceremonial building with all the details of a major structure, from colonnade to forecourt.

ated from molds of those original doors). The penthouse gives the otherwise simple building a pyramidal shape for all its rectangularity and makes for a quietly modern profile.

Inside, the space is spare yet quite luxuriously detailed in keeping with its older sibling, the Library of Congress proper. The lobby features especially delicately colored marble and patented bronze detail, a wise metalwork owl providing a memorable and a bit intimidating bit of metaphor.

The reading room is lofty and carefully lit so as not to create a distraction, the only decoration being the murals that face

War Memorial Building, Jackson, Mississippi, 1939, column capital.

each other across the room and span the entire second story above a stone colonnade. The masonry joints, clearly expressed to be a visible component of the design, add to the overall sense of soundness and quiet.

The War Memorial Building in Jackson, Mississippi, built in 1939–1940, uses a free-standing set of singular columns at the façade for a monumental effect, creating an interior courtyard flanked by the three wings of the building.

The courtyard is truly a court of honor and makes the experience of entering also an experience of remaining outdoors. The memorial houses some amazing sculptural reliefs and a series of cast aluminum plaques that extol war heroes. The capitals are unique in this era for their carved symbolic and art deco faces.

The opposite in look and style can be glimpsed at one of the more exuberant examples of classical modernity, the Saint Paul City Hall in Minnesota, built in 1930–1932. Though not completely unique in using a tower instead of the dome—this form was earlier used in the Nebraska State Capitol and Kansas City's City Hall—the building form was still uncommon for a state capitol building or city hall.

In the Saint Paul building, the architects used the true moderne with strong ties to the true art deco. With a series of angular pylons that frame the main entrance, the complex is a symmetrical composition with a vertical element rising unadorned and makes for a very modern form that was more skyscraper than temple.

The tower's verticality is further emphasized by the bold shadows of the massing and the unadorned piers of the tower's façade. Uncluttered with decoration, the

St. Paul City Hall and Ramsey County Courthouse, Saint Paul, Minnesota, 1932, Lobby. Materials were lux and everywhere used with abandon, yet the effect is almost one of a sacred space rather than civic.

St. Paul City Hall and Ramsey County Courthouse, Saint Paul, Minnesota, 1932, lobby. A little relief from the high drama of the main lobby. The space is secondary but even the lighting standards give a sense of the scenic.

massive main entrance and the scale of the tower show its links to the modern as well as the moderne. However once past the imposing entrance pylons, you find yourself in the epitome of the streamlined moderne style.

With rich materials and theatrical forms it shouts the more extreme manifestations of true art deco. All is perpendicular as matching sets of angular, highly veined, black marble piers rise past pendants of glass and bronze, the effect being akin to the foyer of New York's Radio City Music Hall. Natural light streams through a double-height window framed in a decorative and geometric grillework, while indirect and fanciful lighting elements mysteriously illumine the space against the dark tone of the marble walls. The space has an almost giddy sense of the modern and for a civic building, it borders on the luxe. In fact, this example is perhaps the most like a set out of Hollywood, with its gleaming interior of measured grandeur and the huge spotlit goddess that rises out of the darkness at its far end.

The columns, or piers, diffuse and reflect the lighting, recalling the standards and light troughs in the Chrysler Building. In fact, the building and its attendant spaces is arguably the most "chic" of the civic buildings, a veritable temple to civic virtues. In this, it is the closest to pure theater, with

St. Paul City Hall and Ramsey County Courthouse, Saint Paul, Minnesota, 1932, façade. A classic moderne small skyscraper with beautifully massed elements and a clear emphasis on the vertical. As contemporary as anything built at the time and still sleekly modern today.

St. Paul City Hall and Ramsey County Courthouse, Saint Paul, Minnesota, 1932, Lobby. Without question , the most exuberantly art deco of all the spaces in this book. A complete chiaroscuro film noir experience.

John W. McCormack Post Office & Courthouse, Boston, 1933, library. Simple geometry in metal and the grid express nicely the function of the room.

John W. McCormack Post Office & Courthouse, Boston, 1933, lobby detail.

John W. McCormack Post Office & Courthouse, Boston, 1933, **entrance façade.** Making an entrance in the early '30s was not just for movie stars. Certainly this grandeur would pass as the decade moved on.

John W. McCormack Post Office & Courthouse, Boston, 1933, **lobby.** The art deco influence is apparent in this building, built at the beginning of the New Deal; the space is a conservative example of the style.

California Library & Courts Building, Sacramento, California, 1928. Designed by the architectural firm Weeks and Day, the building exemplifies West Coast grandeur at any cost; notice the columns supporting light urns.

a two-story, carved white marble symbolic figure as its main focal point.

Another high-rise building of the era with a similar decorative exuberance is the McCormack Post Office and Courthouse in Boston. The entrance portals are covered in symbolic, highly carved ornamental devices, while the interior space, painted in colorful designs and lined with warmtoned, engaged marble piers, is both dignified and à la mode. This is a soaring example of civic verticality at its most decorative.

Some buildings held to the older classicism but with a new look. We see this at

Oregon State Capitol, Salem, Oregon, 1938. Certainly one of the most iconic of the era's civic buildings—an ode to the Greek in streamlined elegance.

James T. Foley US Post Office & Courthouse, Albany, New York, 1934, carving on façade. A simplified bas-relief that is almost Egyptian in flatness and which acts as a decorative cornice to the simply and elegantly proportioned building.

the Oregon State Capitol, completed in 1938, with its flattened drum in place of a dome, and in the lobby or memorial entrance vestibule of California's Library & Courts Building of 1928 (a pre-WPA building), where the theater of Saint Paul's City Hall is matched, though here with eight pairs of huge double-height black-marble Doric columns that hold up nothing more than large urns.

Less theatrical but no less impressive is the Foley Courthouse in Albany, New York, a large cubic mass of white marble. Its perfect proportions and refinement mask its size and the sensitive detailing make the building approachable. The mass of the building is softened by the modern wall reliefs and framing of the window piers.

James T. Foley US Post Office & Courthouse, Albany, New York, 1934, façade. An elegant expression of the grand portal smoothly worked into the design.

James T. Foley US Post Office & Courthouse, Albany, New York, 1934, main hall. A beautiful use of contrasting marble to create a sense of rhythm and richness.

James T. Foley US Post Office & Courthouse, Albany, New York, 1934, lighting detail.

James T. Foley US Post Office & Courthouse, Albany, New York, 1934, lobby.

James T. Foley US Post Office & Courthouse, Albany, New York, 1934, detail. Throughout the building, attention to detail and its quality were always considered.

James T. Foley US Post Office & Courthouse, Albany, New York, 1934. Certainly, a sufficient amount of reserve to satisfy the needs of jurisprudence.

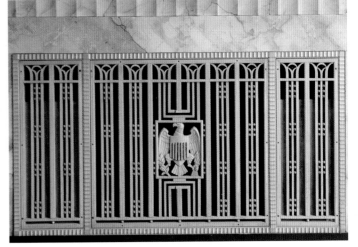

James T. Foley US Post Office & Courthouse, Albany, New York, 1934, decorative grille.

James T. Foley US Post Office & Courthouse, Albany, New York, 1934, detail.

William R. Cotter Federal Building, Hartford, Connecticut, 1933, roof-line eagle. Another eagle has landed less stylized and more in keeping the classic feel of the building.

William R. Cotter Federal Building, Hartford, Connecticut, 1933, façade.

William R. Cotter Federal Building, Hartford, Connecticut, 1933, facade. A bit of imperial Rome in Hartford, the Cotter building retains vestiges of the classic.

Its subtle and appropriate décor set into the white marble adds to the effect of a carved solid and the use of the bas-relief encircling the façades as an animated frieze gives decorative emphasis. The Foley Courthouse stretches out comfortably in a series of pilasters that gently step inwards to frame the expanse of window bays. These recessed bays denote the postal section of the building and unite the two end pavilions where sculptural decoration and a slight change in plane express the dual lobbies.

It is a magnificent building whose interiors are lit by both hanging chandeliers in a modern federal style as well as a very à la mode linear light fixture that is worked into the geometry in the courthouse lobby.

William R. Cotter Federal Building, Hartford, Connecticut, 1933, hall. Long and light, the main postal hall is a well-conceived, simple space with lighting fixtures that establish a sense of rhythm.

William R. Cotter Federal Building, Hartford, Connecticut, 1933, detail, clock.

William R. Cotter Federal Building, Hartford, Connecticut, 1933, floor motif.

William R. Cotter Federal Building, Hartford, Connecticut, 1933, chandelier.

US Custom House, Philadelphia, Pennsylvania, 1934, lobby. The extravagant use of marble and color makes this space, with its coved lighting and dome, a suitable Fred and Ginger set.

US Custom House, Philadelphia, Pennsylvania, 1934, lobby rotunda stairs. Continuing the round theme , the circular stairs are visually arresting and balance the circular room they are pendant to.

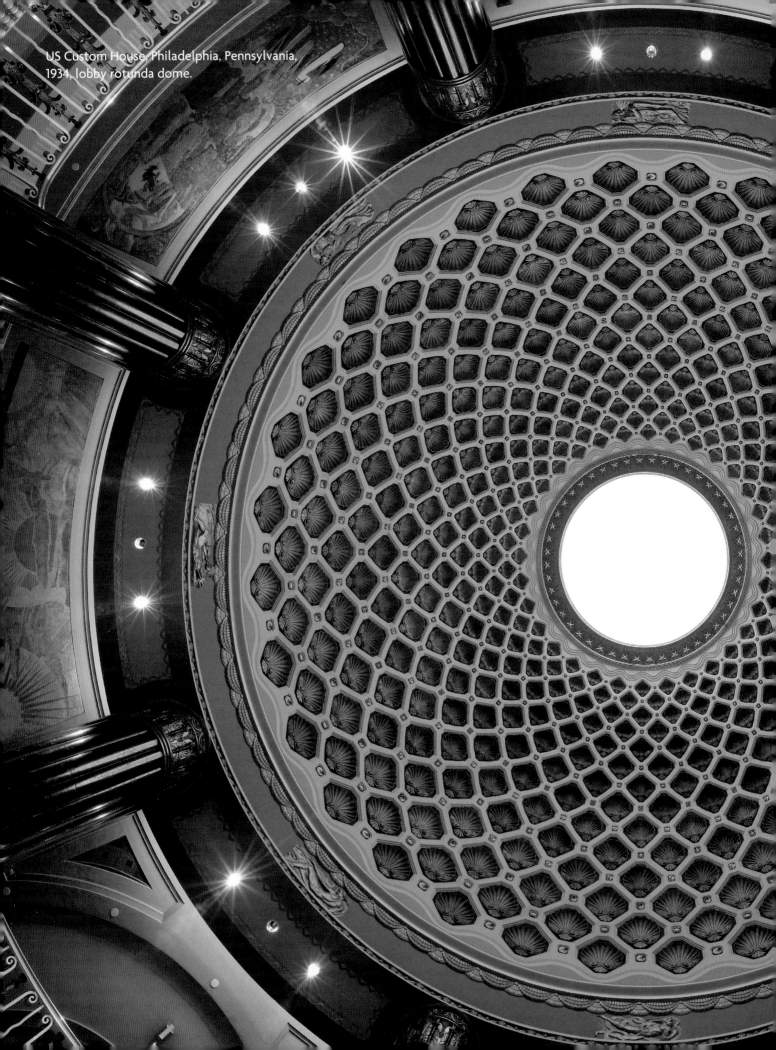

US Custom House, Philadelphia, Pennsylvania, 1934, lobby rotunda dome.

US Custom House, Philadelphia, Pennsylvania, 1934, lobby and rotunda.

The diffused light softens the striking yellow sienna and black marble.

The Cotter Federal Building and Courthouse in Hartford, Connecticut, is the Foley's contemporary and has a similar formal interior spatial arrangement modified by moderne detailing. However, the flanking eagles perched on the parapet of its roof line give the Cotter court an edge in the first-impression category. Though it was built right before FDR was elected, its overall design aesthetic was cited as a model for the WPA to use in its successive federal building projects. All its elements would be adapted and streamlined by the New Deal and its builders. It represents the germinal point of departure for the federal moderne style to take off from.

The ever-present hall that runs the spine of the building is simple and measured by flat, slightly raised columns and original art deco grilles set into the marble wall panes for visual interest.

The interior hall ceiling of the Cotter building is made up of recessed trays from which hang chandeliers of chrome that give the uncluttered, cleanly detailed space a focal point that is continuous. The floor is set with an amusing pattern that alludes to the mail and is a light touch in the civically minded building. The treatment of the giant order of columns framing each

US Custom House, Philadelphia, Pennsylvania, 1934, entrance doors.

entrance and the freestanding sculptures of the American eagle give the building its monumental effect.

In contrast, in the Philadelphia United States Custom House, simplicity gives way to the pleasure of circles and curves. Highly colored marbles and cast aluminum panels offer a glimpse of the moderne world via a form that is more tied to the art deco jazziness of the previous decade. This is a long way from the simplicity of the Nix building, but it illustrates the parameters of the style and the various degrees of opulence that could be used under the WPA banner. The building is something

of a hybrid in its mixed design metaphors, including attributes of Philadelphia federalist architecture mixed with the federal moderne. Once inside, however, the aesthetic language changes.

This interior space is in the tradition of Boston's McCormack: it is pure art deco in its series of foyers and halls, its walls painted and bronzed, leading to a circular rotunda that is the centerpiece of the building. Surfaces are all very highly colored and activated. The main design theme is circular and to stand under the rotunda is to be in an uncornered universe of rich materials and color.

The expansive feeling is heightened by the pair of flanking circular stairs leading to the mezzanine level.

Surrounding the central space is a ring of highly polished convexly fluted black marble columns with simplified gilded capitals and bases. The metal decorative panels and rails are aluminum and monometal, used for the whiteness of color and reflective qualities. This space would be at home in any large urban center as a theater or skyscraper of the roaring '20s. No expense seemed to be spared on the overall effect of colorful dignity with a moderne curve!

Federal Courthouse (William Kenzo Nakamura US Courthouse), Seattle, Washington, 1940, façade. With an emphasis on mass and verticality, this building is most indicative of the latter WPA style as well as the shape of things to come.

Federal Courthouse (William Kenzo Nakamura US Courthouse), Seattle, Washington, 1940, window detail. A typical window treatment of the time, where the window bays seem cut into the surface plain.

Federal Courthouse (William Kenzo Nakamura US Courthouse), Seattle, Washington, 1940, court. A very beautiful room, two stories tall and lit by windows that relate elegantly with the exterior fenestration.

Federal Courthouse (William Kenzo Nakamura US Courthouse), Seattle, Washington, 1940, façades. Another view that shows the bulk of the building beautifully softened by the rhythm of the windows, the square, smaller top floor acting almost as capitals to the implied pillars.

Chapter Seven: The New Deal Moves Ahead
The Calm Before the Storm

Detroit Federal Building & US Courthouse (now, Theodore Levin US Courthouse), 1934, façade. Built earlier than the Seattle Federal building, its massing is similar though the window bays are broken and the general composition of the façade more scattered.

Detroit Federal Building & US Courthouse (now, Theodore Levin US Courthouse), 1934, carving on façade. The wall reliefs act as a defining cornice that break the height just over midway, followed by a subtle setback and change of window rhythm.

By mid-decade, the new style and the New Deal were no longer novel. One was a way of building, while the other was a way of life for many Americans. A war was looming in Europe, and in spite of the various world's fairs and expositions aimed at lifting spirits and looking ahead to the future, such as New York's World's Fair of 1939, a totalitarian sentiment was moving across Europe and the world.

I sometimes wonder if the increasingly fortress-like qualities that one begins to see in buildings in the years prior to our entry into the war is a reaction to this feeling of conflict. With an increasing abstraction into lights and darks, the structures assumed a more contemporary, rather than classic, format. The change was one of proportions. Where earlier, more formulaic buildings expressed the internal divisions of the building's interior more directly, one could still easily make out the positioning of the main hall or court by the relative size of the windows and their décor. As the structures increased in size, the vertical elements became less like piers in the classic sense, becoming instead vertical cuts into the flat plane of the building. Dark verticals pierce the white marble façades, achieving a form of proto-minimal art if one looks at the plane of the wall as a painting.

Aside from the few buildings that still used the forms and templates with the florid and colorful ornamental devices of the earlier, more decorative period, by the

Detroit Federal Building & US Courthouse (now, Theodore Levin US Courthouse), 1934, detail. Carving of the ubiquitous eagle at the entrance, surmounting a pilaster as its capital.

Detroit Federal Building & US Courthouse (now, Theodore Levin US Courthouse), 1934, main hall. A large and long space with arched ceiling, adding a touch of the grand to the simple detailing.

beginning of the war, this style had all but disappeared in civic architecture and design.

The façade of the Seattle US Courthouse, an arrangement in light and dark, devoid of external ornament as well as any hint of the decoration within, has a clean almost antiseptic feeling. With its lack of carved or painted décor, partially a result of the troubled times, the interior public space became more office-like and shed in the process any allusions of civic grandeur save for the beautiful and tall bronze grilles that frame the double-height windows of the courts in quiet geometry.

Seattle, as well as any number of projects that were able to be completed during wartime when materials and men were scarce for civic construction, was built in 1940, one of the last big boxes built as the world turned to war, and its fortress-like presence seems designed more to defend than recover.

Detroit's Federal Building and US Courthouse of 1934 is an earlier manifestation of this form and used a similar abstract arrangement of solid and void, but the exterior also has a carved frieze depicting the work of the automobile industry. The frieze shows a change in the pattern of the window openings' fenestration and its imagery of auto workers lends a human element, which aids in softening the angularity of the building.

Federal Building and US Courthouse, Peoria, Illinois, 1938, façade. Long and asymmetrical, the interior functions are easily discerned. The decoration is more reticent than what might be expected for such a large building.

Federal Building and US Courthouse, Peoria, Illinois, 1938, façade. A large building announces its sense of importance to the community. The central bay projects forward enough to read as a colonnade, adding focus to the fairly unadorned façade.

Federal Building and US Courthouse, Peoria, Illinois, 1938, lobby. A long space helped by its height as well as the windows, expressed on the façade, that flood the room with light.

Federal Building and US Courthouse, Peoria, Illinois, 1938, court. A smart and lovely room where the proportions work beautifully with the official scale of the space.

Federal Building and US Courthouse, Peoria, Illinois, 1938, detail, court. Throughout the court, first-rate materials are used. The federal moderne design is elegant and understated.

The interior is still grand with its softly curving ceiling and indirect lighting and rich colors and materials. All of the decorative elements are quietly present, in line with the general understatement used in the design.

When the moderne gave way to the modern is truly when this form of high-rise civic building took its ascendency in civic architecture.

The trend had an effect on the many decorative and fine artists who were once needed to enhance the exterior and interior of these buildings, but the war more than likely took care of the employment problem. Earlier buildings like the Peoria, Illinois, and Sioux City, Iowa, federal buildings had employed carvers and stone masons to adorn the façades and interior spaces. Columns might be reduced to mere fluting or vertical incisions in the stone but elements such as the capital, now a flat geometry, needed to be carved or cast.

For a decade, measured and solid façades,

Federal Building and US Courthouse, Sioux City, Iowa, 1934, façade. A large building whose intelligent decoration gives it a more human scale.

Federal Building and US Courthouse, Sioux City, Iowa, 1934, façade. The entrance bay projects just enough to become a central pavilion and breaks the march of vertical window bays across the long façade.

Federal Building and US Courthouse, Sioux City, Iowa, 1934, façade. Hardly a break in the wall plane to define the entrance, which also serves as a sort of tower.

Federal Building and US Courthouse, Sioux City, Iowa, 1934, lobby. A dignified but somewhat cold interior, probably due to the use of white marble to clad almost everything structural.

Federal Building and US Courthouse, Sioux City, Iowa, 1934, light standard. Four-square as the building, its lighting standards announce the entrance and show the quality of the material.

Federal Building and US Courthouse, Sioux City, Iowa, 1934, stair hall. A fine **example of** decorative metalwork of the interwar years, modern yet decorative to hold the interest of the visitor beyond mere function.

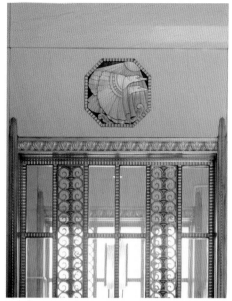

Federal Building and US Courthouse, Sioux City, Iowa, 1934, window detail.

Federal Building and US Courthouse, Sioux City, Iowa, 1934, ceiling.

Austin US Courthouse, Austin, Texas, 1934, façade. A similar profile to the Sioux City Federal Building, though perhaps a less successful attempt at emphasis.

such as those seen on the federal buildings in Peoria and Sioux City, were the standard. Though the interiors might be formulaic and strictly business, there was always a sense of quality of material and workmanship as evidenced by the beauty of Sioux City, its façade an example of the skillful use of vertical piers emphasizing height and also lateral progression, all within a set framework of light and dark. The interior of cream marble walls and white sim-

plified pilasters is hardly one to stir the imagination, but the beautiful and original grillework and details, such as the shining bronze star motifs, keep the spaces from being too severe.

The US Courthouse in Austin, completed in 1935, has a more pre-Depression abandon in its use of decoration and details. The sweeping curve of the grand marble and aluminum stairs and the highly ornamental sets of brass and black lacquered

doors clearly speak of their art deco roots. With its swelling curves, the projecting central pavilion manages to imply a portico without any columns. The main façade and central section are simply detailed and minimal. The judicial wing is defined by the series of sculpted panels that are set below the main courtroom's double-height windows.

But by 1938, when the Peoria Federal Building was finished, the minimalist move

Austin US Courthouse, Austin, Texas, 1935, façade. A compact structure with fairly standard fenestration, the discreet carving at the roof-line gives a more finished look.

Austin US Courthouse, Austin, Texas, 1935, stair.

had started to integrate with the earlier forms. Looking at this building, a shift in the proportions and distribution of mass was already being seen. Perhaps due to its great length, this building needed the relief from the rows of vertical piers expressed as columns. In effect, the rhythm is broken by the shifts of the various parts.

With Peoria, we have the two design conventions in mid-stream, a move from the decorative to the sleek. The interior main hall, an almost minimal space, relies on its materials to give it a sense of civic use. The ceiling is treated as a series of recessed receding squares with decoratively gilded geometric designs inset beneath each window.

Austin US Courthouse, Austin, Texas, 1935, door to court.

Austin US Courthouse, Austin, Texas, 1935, detail, clock.

Austin US Courthouse, Austin, Texas, 1935, detail, doors.

Austin US Courthouse, Austin, Texas, 1935, stair.

Chapter Eight: The Buck Stopped Here and There
The Aesthetic Legacy of the New Deal

Department of Interior, Washington, DC, 1936 Where it all began—home of the all the various programs of the New Deal, and a repository of much of the best of the period's art.

In a world about to ignite, these buildings were symbolic of the safe harbor the federal government hoped to keep the country moored in. With their sheer wall planes and simplified fenestration they are more fortress than temple. From the purely art deco federalism of the early '30s to these austere examples of the last years of the decade, the WPA style of federal moderne was total.

It was FDR himself who, when asked about the programs he started, said that the WPA would be remembered for its art and architecture. These words were prescient!

The buildings that were designed and built during this troubled ten-year period reflect the sober and difficult times the country was trying to escape. From the famous to the unknown, artists were called on to make paintings and sculpture that would be integrated into these spaces.

The symbolic home of this new style was the Department of the Interior Building in Washington, DC, a huge, white mass of stone and courtyards where FDR and his cadre of bureaucrats created the WPA/PWA alphabet soup programs. This building houses a collection of murals that are a worthy of any museum of American art and have been lovingly preserved and documented fully by the GSA.

It is truly here that FDR's words ring with a sharp peal.

The Department of the Interior Building is certainly the largest of the WPA architectural constructs in terms of sheer size. An absolutely mind-boggling structure, it is really six buildings that cover two full city blocks. What is striking is the way this enormous solid cube of a building achieves its intended purpose as an office and yet creates the feeling of a community. The building, for all its impassive exterior walls,

has a modulated massing that saves it from monotony. Aside from the simple but well-executed and chaste exterior décor, the Interior Building relies on the shadows and voids created by the repetition of the six main elements or wings. These voids seem to have been carved out of one vast block of stone; the constantly shifting angles of light and dark activate its many façades and keep the building from feeling overwhelming.

Sited on a slope, the building has essentially two main entrances, as well as two lobbies on different floors.

The south entrance, one story above the north, links the most prominent of the floors or lobbies with great ease through Grand Stair Hall directly in the middle of the structure. After what is essentially a long and wide "indoor street" of one story comes this sudden spatial change, relieving the axial progression and giving the feeling

Department of the Interior, Washington, DC, 1936, façade. Detail of the entrance façade with its screen of square piers that soften the huge mass of the building.

Department of the Interior, Washington, DC, 1936, lobby. Fine marble and bronze enhance the otherwise sober lobby; a corresponding space is on the opposite end of the building.

Department of the Interior, Washington, DC, 1936, hall and lighting.

Department of the Interior, Washington, DC, 1936, stair. Main stairwell leading to the lower lobby and entrance; it gives a sense of grand space to an otherwise very long corridor that runs the building's length.

Department of the Interior, Washington, DC, 1936, stair.

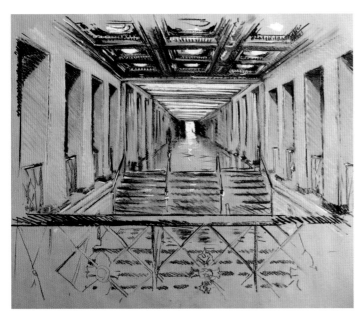

Department of the Interior, Washington, DC, 1936, stair hall, painting by the author.

Department of the Interior, Washington, DC, 1936, entrance. The vestibule beneath the columned section and the entry to the building; this is one of two entrances on different levels, due to the slope of the site.

of rising or descending to a continuous vanishing point. This is modified with checkered marble floors and lateral vistas of color in its murals, which are its glory and only real decoration. Each section of the hall is divided by shallow trays of light concealed in the perimeter cornice. The effect of these light "cubes" receding down the long space helps to control the distant vista.

At the Department of the Interior Building, we are not so much dealing with a lobby space as a grand thoroughfare bisecting the building laterally and, at the Grand Stair, vertically.

Department of the Interior, Washington, DC, 1936, cafeteria mural. Much wall space was given over to Native American themes, and there was a complete Indian shop on the premises when the building opened in 1936.

Department of the Interior, Washington, DC, 1936, auditorium.

Department of the Interior, Washington, DC, 1936, auditorium.

The conference hall, or auditorium, is located off the foyer and is a large and classically detailed WPA space of double height with rows of simplified fluted Doric piers on each side, forming aisles for a basilica-type plan. Flanking the stage are carved decorative panels of stone. The room and columns are in a buff limestone with white marble wainscoting and base. The capitals and details are lightly gilded and bronzed. As the room is two stories, it is surrounded by a balcony, lit with clerestory windows and decorated with carved reliefs. The stage has a huge carved eagle over the square proscenium and once had a large mural on the back wall that has since been moved.

It is one of the grandest of the Interior spaces in terms of architectural presence. Along with the cafeteria and its Indian-in-

spired murals, the auditorium is also one of the largest spaces of the Interior and occupies an entire wing. Also on this floor and occupying the lateral wing is the Library, another double-height room on a smaller scale. All metalwork and carvings are finely wrought and finished as is the entire detailing of the structure.

Among the works of art that decorate the halls and rooms are two large reliefs of bison and moose that flank the first-floor landing as part of the approach to the central stair and give importance to the long space leading to it.

Among the notable artists whose works decorate the halls are Millard Sheets, William Gropper, Ernest Fiene, and John Stuart Curry, with techniques that vary

from mural to fresco.

The real treasures of the building are its wonderful collection of WPA murals, painted expressly for the halls and as decorations for the various public spaces (see chapter nine for more about the WPA murals). The sober and understated approach to the decoration shows how a quality structure can be truly grand and simple.

Centered on the axis of the building, the Grand Stair occupies the full width of the main corridor rising two full stories to a coffered ceiling. Surrounding the second floor of the stairs is a gallery composed of eight paired, square muscular piers that create an aisle for circulation around the center well.

Department of the Interior, Washington, DC, 1936, cafeteria mural. The vast space of one of the courtyards roofed originally in glass for use as the cafeteria for the employees.

Department of the Interior, Washington, DC, 1936, mural.

Department of the Interior, Washington, DC, 1936, mural at end of hallway. Iconic image of the construction of a dam by Edward Gropper; this is perhaps his best-known work and indicative of WPA-style painting.

This idea of using the mural to expand the somewhat confined space of the Interior is used to great effect on the upper floors where, due to the length of the corridor, the sense of infinity is alleviated by a wall of murals at either end as well as decorative sets of carved doors at various points.

Some of the central halls of the Interior building have, at their ends, large, floor-to-ceiling murals by some by the most important painters of American art. These works were intended for the enjoyment of the federal employees working in this vast network of halls and spaces. The work has been spaced out over the entire structure in key places on each floor. As one travels the building from north to south, the element of surprise is established. You know that when you reach the end of a hall, there will be a visual treat to greet you. This integration of art and the workplace is germane to the WPA goal of connecting enrichment with employment.

Department of the Interior, Washington, DC, 1936, mural.

Federal Trade Commission Building (originally, Apex Building), Washington, DC, 1938, façade. Understated and restrained neoclassic moderne, with an emphasis on classic. The building does contain some lovely details that speak to the period such as the metalwork and wonderful carvings, such as the corner colonnade.

Federal Trade Commission Building (originally, Apex Building), Washington, DC, 1938, entry. Main entry with aluminum doors that refer to commerce and the iconic carving of workers over the door.

Federal Trade Commission Building (originally, Apex Building), Washington, DC, 1938, stair.

Federal Trade Commission Building (originally, Apex Building), Washington, DC, 1938, grille.

Federal Trade Commission Building (originally, Apex Building), Washington, DC, 1938, statue.

US Department of Justice Building (Robert F. Kennedy Building), Washington, DC, 1935, hall to library. Surely one of the most elegant and sophisticated of all the spaces in this book.

US Department of Justice Building (Robert F. Kennedy Building), Washington, DC, 1935, entrance lobby.

Although there were in America, at the time of the WPA, artists who were true moderns, such as Eliel Saarinen, who worked in architecture and design, and Stuart Davis, who painted uniquely American forms of abstraction, these artists were not generally called upon for public commissions of this stature. The prevailing aesthetic was a North American and very sober style of representation. It is a style based in part on the "honesty" of the American spirit and its effects on the plastic arts. In America, it was the past as a living history.

Another very large and quietly detailed Washington, DC, building of the same period is the Federal Trade Commission Building, originally called the Apex building when it was completed in 1938. Instead of the continuous march of the Interior Building, Apex gets its individuality from a circular colonnade that forms the building's apex, from which the name was derived. Aside from this prominent piece of staging, it is a no-nonsense building whose size belies the simplicity of its interior. The modern stair hall and lobby grilles have an almost Bauhaus-like severity.

In the nation's capital, the space that is truly definitive of the WPA style at its most rich and thoughtful is the fifth-floor Grand Hall and lobby of the Department of Justice where one sees the important decorative role murals play when considered as part of a total design, both in terms of décor and the meaning of the space.

There is a certain homogeneity about the work found in most of the major federal projects that easily identifies them as part of the New Deal, and the DOJ building is no exception and is in fact a paradigm.

The intricacy of the lobby space with its lateral galleries and stairwell opening off a truly grand hall is in the finest of classical moderne taste. In fact, the building itself is in the traditional Washington neoclassic style, albeit more simplified, but does make use of modern materials, especially the then-new aluminum for decorative and functional purposes. The twenty-foot-tall entrance doors are made of cast

US Department of Justice Building (Robert F. Kennedy Building), Washington, DC, 1935, fifth-floor lobby. The fifth-floor lobby to the Law Library is a space where no expense was spared in materials and workmanship as well as artistic choices.

US Department of Justice Building (Robert F. Kennedy Building), Washington, DC, 1935, elevator hall.

and worked aluminum that retract into the walls when open; their motifs are a very simple geometric meander. Flanking the entrance bays are tall lighting standards in a typical art deco form that relate to the moderne of the doors but contrast oddly with the exterior details.

Inside the Grand Hall space, the wonderful lighting that seems to glow produces an otherworldly sensation, almost religious. Above, the aluminum-leafed ceiling, ringed by a decorative frieze of abstracted forms, is bathed in warm light from coffers hidden in the cornice that encircles the room. The reflected light from the ceiling

is enough to bathe the murals at either end in soft light.

The lobby is actually a series of interrelated spaces. Screens of columns frame the Law Library entrance and a second foyer and stairwell. The regularly spaced and fluted pilasters without capitals or bases are carved in warm toned stone that tempers the otherwise cool feel of the space, an effect heightened by the aluminum-leafed ceiling and encircling frieze.

The stairs are incorporated into the design by the colorful mural decoration as seen through a screen of square, fluted piers that separate the stairwell from the

main space. The lighting throughout the Grand Hall is consistent, reflected, and even. It is a very complex space, held together by light and the color of the murals whose subject matter is judicial, with special regard to equality and civil rights.

With the DOJ building, a definite high point of interior design and the WPA style of federalist modernity was achieved. Throughout the decade, many such buildings were constructed under the aegis of the WPA and what we have seen in this book is but a small sampling of those owned and maintained by the federal government. They were a product of the times and of

US Department of Justice Building (Robert F. Kennedy Building), Washington, DC, 1935, mural.

the hope FDR extended to maintain a future America despite the nation's economic and then political troubles.

The war came, and with it, the emphasis on style and design disappeared. The legacy that remains is a fascinating group of buildings that tell us about an era and the country's efforts to give America a New Deal. The federal programs and laws passed then have grown into the system that we live and work under today. The buildings that were designed to trumpet the social changes of the New Deal still stand as beacons of America's glory. They remind us of our architectural heritage and also our social history and progress.

US Department of Justice Building (Robert F. Kennedy Building), Washington, DC, 1935, sculpture.

Chapter Nine: The WPA and the Art of the Mural

The Meaning of Social Security, Ben Shahn, 1941, Oil, detail, Wilbur J. Cohen Federal Building, (former Social Security Building) Washington, DC.

The real heart of the New Deal was its art, inseparable, if only in spirit, from the buildings the art was made for and from the epoch in which the pieces were created.

The Charles Wells mural *The New Deal,* created for the Clarkson S. Fisher Federal Building and US Courthouse in Trenton, New Jersey, for example, speaks volumes of the trying times facing so many citizens during the '30s. In the expressions on the faces of the toiling workers and the colors of the earth, Wells captured the moment in time when Americans desperately needed a New Deal!

With his New Deal Franklin D. Roosevelt made a commitment to bring the country out of the Depression as well as to uplift the spirits of a public so vanquished by the trying times. The visual example of this achievement was the construction and embellishment of federal building projects throughout the country and in the nation's capital. The WPA and PWA, along with various other new government departments, were committed to this embellishment, which guaranteed the livelihood of artists and the creation of many great works of art. That art, and especially the mural, was to play a central role in this aesthetic propaganda. Just as the architecture submitted itself to the cause of the Republic, so too did these murals and decorations. In the best painterly tradition, the artists stepped up to the plate and delivered the social and civic ball game in aesthetics that ran the gamut of a particular style of American painting.

New Deal, Charles Wells, 1933, *Oil, 10' x 6',* Clarkson S. Fisher Federal Building, Trenton, NJ.

The pictures have a homogeneity indicative of the times in which they were made, with its ideals and its difficulties.

The art of the '30s had a job to do that went beyond pure décor. Just as the new architecture was designed to express the feeling of American strength and wellness, so too were these pictures. Uplifting and imbued with patriotic zeal, a mural was the tried-and-true way to add visual interest and dignity to civic space. Any wall in every civic building was a potential home for a bit of American art that showed the history of or daily happenings in American life in simple and elegant form and color, as does Ben Shahn's *The Meaning of Social Security* multi-panel mural in the old Social

Security Administration Building, now the Wilbur J. Cohen Federal Building. Almost every aspect of everyday life is touched upon in this mural created for a building where government workers toiled to secure that way of life.

Everyday life is also a theme in the frescoes at the Department of Justice. The murals here offer not just representations of law but also a glimpse of real American family life, perhaps tidied up a bit, but certainly unvarnished enough to create some sense of empathy. The enormous space of the stair hall is broken up into segments that George Biddle united by color and compositional device in the five-panel mural *Society Freed Through*

Society Freed Through Justice, George Biddle, year?, *Fresco, detail,* Department of Justice Building, Washington, DC.

Society Freed Through Justice, George Biddle, year?, *Fresco, detail,* Department of Justice Building, Washington, DC.

Pony Express, Frank Mechau, 1937, *Oil, 7' x 13',* Department of the Interior Building, Washington, DC.

Justice. Though segmented, the panels are unified by their narrative theme. This sectioning of the main storyline is not uncommon and was used most evocatively in Frank Mechau's *Pony Express* mural for the Post Office Building (now the Wil-liam Jefferson Clinton Federal Building) amongst other commissions.

The tradition of wall painting in public buildings is a long one, and during the interwar years, the mural underwent a stylistic change. Instead of following the classical ideal, artists turned to the present and the theme of the human condition, interpreting familiar themes through a contemporary lens. Looking at Ezra Winter's *Canterbury Tales* murals in the North Reading Room of the Library of Congress

Canterbury Tales, Ezra Winter, 1939, *Oil, detail,* Library Of Congress, John Adams Building, Washington, DC.

Entry Into the Forest, Candido Portinari, 1939, *Tempera,* Library of Congress , John Adams Building, Washington, DC.

and then the Candido Portinari murals for the same building's Hispanic Reading Room, one sees clearly a difference in style and feeling. While the Winter mural is a chaste and somber frieze, the Brazilian-born Portinari captures all the color in jewel tones and patterns in *Entry into the Forest.* The New World becomes a sparkling narrative of discovery with much hubris of hue. Winter's work is a more retro, illustrative style, while Porinari—though showing an event from history—gives his piece a timeless immediacy and is more in keeping with the modern aesthetic.

Even in John Steuart Curry's 1939 straightforward rendition of a historic event, *Oklahoma Land Rush, April 22, 1889,* one senses a certain newness of style and timeliness in the rush of people, animals, wagons, and a bicycle.

Wall paintings became a form of civic entertainment on par with a visit to a gallery. The average American could have exposure to contemporary art with just a visit to the local post office or courthouse. The mural was an art form for the people—as abstract expressionist Arshile Gorky dismissively noted, "poor art for poor people." His was an elitist view, shared by many Americans of the upper classes who felt the political and social realism of civic art was too mainstream. However, the "mainstream" was what needed the entertainment, and they did not want something unfamiliar and outside their immediate comprehension. The step away from the

Oklahoma Land Rush, John Steuart Curry, 1939, *Oil, 109" x 235",* Department of the Interior Building, Washington, DC.

commonplace into the area of abstraction and surreal was a bit too steep for most Americans, and so it was to regionalist and social realist artists like Reginald Marsh and John Steuart Curry that the New Deal turned to visualize the American zeitgeist. These artists held to a narrative in their work and many were associated with the labor and social movements of the times. It has been said that many of the murals handled themes of labor and justice with adroitness because most of the artists were socialists. That certainly would have been true of some of the artists working for the WPA. For the important federal projects, artists were selected to compete. The winners of those competitions were then commissioned to do the work, rather than being hired by the government.

The PWA commissioned art that was not only considered accessible but also high minded. It was to speak explicitly of American values and mores. A populist vision of the American scene, it had to be one that was inspiring. The mural held a special place in the American psyche, representing high ideals.

Unfortunately, in the post–World War II years, the genre fell from favor. Propaganda was no longer needed to spur on the populace. The television would soon come of age and visual imagery turned toward the mediums of film and camera. Even the photo mural was considered too "illustra-

tive," which, by the '50s was anathema to modern art. Many of the civic structures and their art were deemed obsolete, too big, or too grand. No one was interested in seeing depictions of toiling laborers when the country was on a roll. During the '50s and '60s much of this art was neglected, or worse, removed entirely.

Were it not for the care and understanding of their historical and artistic value by the Department of the Interior, many of these works of art would have been lost forever instead of being carefully removed from their sites and stored for safekeeping. Some of the works have been unseen by the general public for decades.

In addition, while most, if not all, of the WPA buildings in Washington are intact, many of the government-owned facilities across the country have been either altered or are no longer in use. The art created for them is inaccessible as well. It is for this reason, in addition to their exemplary quality, that I focus in this chapter on murals in the nation's capital.

Fortunately, in recent years, public opinion about WPA art has begun to change again, spurred by the purchase of Thomas Hart Benton's *America Today* murals by AXA (Equitable Life) in 1984. Originally painted for the New School for Social Research in New York City, the insurance company restored the ten-panel mural and in 1996 put it on display in its new lobby

on Avenue of the Americas. The notoriety this engendered in the art world, as well as in the popular consciousness, was immediate. All of a sudden the New Deal and WPA were back in the public eye. (In 2012, the mural was donated to the Metropolitan Museum of Art.)

The renewed interest in this long-overlooked American art underlines the current work on the part of the GSA to resurrect orphaned and sequestered works. Kept in storage or behind closed doors, these visual cues to our past are being brought to light again.

I am sure as interest grows, the murals will find their proper place in the history of American art of the Depression years.

The Selection Process

The federal buildings erected during the WPA era make Washington, DC, one of the great repositories of WPA/PWA art.

Good buildings can inform the aesthetic idea of space and form, but essentially they are mute. In that respect, it is their decoration, their painting and sculpture, that gives them their voice and makes for a dialogue between the whole and what it stood for—the American spirit, so battered during the '30s.

This is an apropos time to clear up a common confusion about "WPA art." This umbrella term is often used to describe

Battle of Trenton, George Wells, 1933, *Oil, detail,* Clarkson S. Fisher Federal Building, Trenton, NJ.

Native Americans, Allan Houser, 1936, *Secco, detail,* Department of the Interior Building, Washington, DC.

and categorize *all* work painted during this time for the federal government. But it is important to distinguish between different programs within the New Deal.

As noted earlier, the New Deal, established in 1933 by the newly elected President Roosevelt, spawned an array of programs, including the Public Works Administration, which was under the direction of Harold Ickes, one of FDR's most trusted appointees and closest of friends. The specific goal of all of the New Deal programs, known by their acronyms, was to provide work for the unemployed of the Depression, and it was Harold Ickes who insisted that this group include artists. The first federal art project was the Public Works of Art

Project (PWAP), which lasted six months and provided work relief for artists. It was followed in 1935 by the Treasury Relief Act, which ran until 1939 and employed 275 artists and was targeted at creating art for decorating federal buildings. A third program, the Works Progress Administration's Federal Art Project (WPA/FAP), which ran from 1935 to 1943, included performing artists and writers and created more than 5,000 jobs for artists. Through these work-relief programs, literally thousands of artists were hired and put to work. Employed by the government, they would continue painting, for the most part, easel pictures, which would ultimately find their way as decorations in various civic build-

ings like hospitals and schools.

The art that emerged from these programs is not the art we came to know as WPA style. The art we are concerned with here would reach its apotheosis in the large-scale and monumental murals of which Wells's huge *Battle of Trenton* is indicative, These works were commissioned by the WPA and by a special Section of Painting and Sculpture program that was established in 1934 under the administration of the United States Department of the Treasury. This program, which would later be known as the Section of Fine Arts, would provide the new federal buildings with their aesthetic heart. Approximately 1 percent of the total cost of construction of these federal buildings was reserved for decoration.

For the more important federal buildings in and out of Washington, the era's more prominent and established artists were asked to compete for the commission of a specific work for a specific site. These were to be paintings that would exemplify the role of the mural as a tool, a form of propaganda, if you will, that would inspire as well as decorate the federal space.

The relatively few artists chosen to receive the important commissions for specific buildings were generally able to make a living from their professional work. The Section not only chose the artist, but then also approved the design of the intended murals. All of the artists chosen to submit proposals and renderings had shown an ability to handle large-scale public work. The murals and sculpture represent the work of some of the most prominent artists practicing during the 1930s in this country, including some truly indigenous artwork of American Indians.

The Section, with its limited staff in Washington, DC, commissioned 1,400 works of art during the life of the program, some of which are among the best examples of mid-twentieth-century American regionalist art. Much of the best New Deal

art can be found intact today in the Interior Department and other Federal buildings in Washington DC., where, though hidden from the general public, they continue to function as both décor and as a reminder of a very particular time in America and the arts.

Several methods were employed in the selection process in commissioning artwork of distinguished quality. Advisory committees with as many as twenty members were formed, with members chosen on the basis of experience and knowledge in the art field. The committee was asked to recommend names of American painters and sculptors whom they felt were particularly qualified to carry out the work in the building in question. Commissions were then awarded through direct appointment by the Section, without contest, based on these recommendations.

Additional artists could be selected to decorate the less prominent space of the larger buildings through an open and anonymous competition that all citizens of the United States were eligible to enter. The advisory committee members were then asked to serve on a special jury that reviewed the submissions. A special goal was commissioning some of the best contemporary Native American artists; these

works eventually covered 2,200 square feet of wall space in the Interior Building, particularly in the cafeteria and the employees lounge. The Bureau of Indian affairs assisted in these selections.

For works that were of lesser importance or were destined for more rural or regional buildings, the artists were chosen by open and anonymous competitions. These competitions, on a state and local level, were open to all citizen artists whose abilities would make them a possible candidate for inclusion in the commission process.

Throughout the process, the submissions were continually evaluated by various juries and committees to make sure that the work of art, either sculpture or mural, had some relationship to the architectural design. These basic qualities would be judged step-by-step as the project moved along.

Subjects and Themes

Themes could vary, but were required to keep within the set strictures laid down by the Section. Themes ranged from history to scenes of social justice, as found in the Department of Justice Building.

Aside from the historical or scientific import, New Deal paintings were generally also to have some uplifting moral or

Consolidation of the West, Ward Lockwood, 1937, Fresco, 109" x 235", William Jefferson Clinton Federal Building (Old Post Office), Washington, DC.

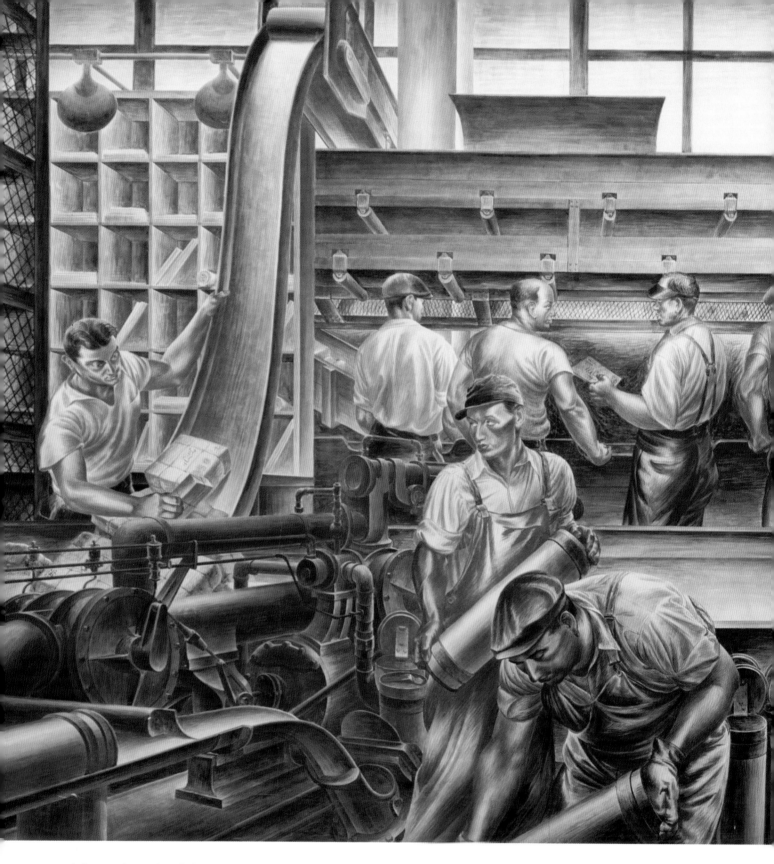

social theme that echoed the American way of life—idealized and smoothed portraits of the people and places of the America of the '30s. In the depths of the financial crisis, when so many were living in reduced circumstances and even poverty, these pictures would carry the idea that we will come through it all, much like a medicine with a calming effect. They would relieve the stress as well as express the way out of it to the citizenry. The national struggle became "our fight," and one that we could win.

National growth and industrialization were often favored in the larger cities. In a smaller city or rural town the storyline might include the history of the area in terms of farming, particularly popular in the Midwest. Western regions often featured paintings that depicted the settlement of the West.

As noted previously, artists chosen were of a realist bent with not a small touch of regionalism. The works also usually bore

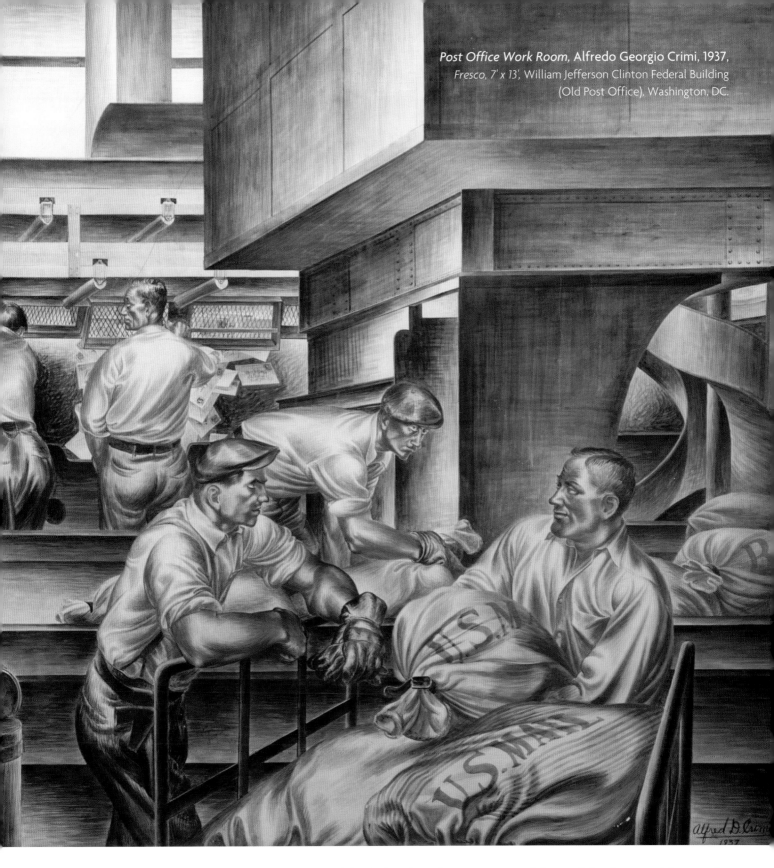

Post Office Work Room, Alfredo Georgio Crimi, 1937,
Fresco, 7' x 13', William Jefferson Clinton Federal Building
(Old Post Office), Washington, DC.

some particular reference to the branch of government whose space the artwork was to occupy. Murals were engaged in active storytelling. To that end, a widely used device was the predella, a series of smaller paintings either below the main subject or on either side that continues the story or theme. Mechau's *Pony Express* and McCosh's

National Parks both show how this creates an almost cinematic effect. In its time, the style was considered quite modern, if not avant-garde. The average Joe, upon entering a civic building in the Midwest or South, was very likely to be greeted with a wall of color that spoke to the origins and geographic necessities of that region.

If destined for the capital district, the paintings did not have to follow any specifically regional idea of place as they were in a more cosmopolitan setting and almost any civic theme or historical event could be a prime subject. Here the paintings could range from subjects as diverse as

Harvest Dance, James Auchiah 1939, *Secco, 96" x 660",*
Department of the Interior Building, Washington, DC.

Transportation of Mail, Alfredo Georgio Crimi,1937, *Fresco, 7' x 13',* William Jefferson Clinton Federal Building (Old Post Office), Washington, DC.

scientific discoveries by great Americans to the grand vistas of the American west.

The Department of the Interior used the mural in its headquarters as a tool to show off the many and varied programs it sponsored for land reclamation and the federal parks, both subjects of civic importance and popular use. Though much less

known today, artists such as Crimi and David McCosh had respectable careers and their pictures bear witness to their powerful talents, the one with his keen sense of the worker, the other with his depictions of the grand space of the western parks and the broken horizon.

Native Americans were popular subjects

for the Department of the Interior building, home to the Bureau of Indian Affairs offices. Apache, Pottawattamie, Kiowa, and Cherokee tribes, among others, can be seen in the wonderful mural at the employees' cafeteria, which has delighted the workers since its installation. In this vast and naturally lit space where both front and rear

Themes of the National Parks, **David McCosh, 1936,** *Oil, 4'6" x 11',* Department of the Interior Building, Washington, DC.

walls are arched, following the curve of the ceiling vault, the American Indians' story is told with color and an immediacy of spirit.

It is interesting to see the equanimity with which the Section viewed both the "pale face" and the Indians and their perspectives on the settlement of the West.

The subtle depictions of Native Americans by Maynard Dixon, done for those offices, are a good example of how American Indians were to be seen in the polished

Bureau of Indian Affairs: Indian & Teacher, Maynard Dixon, 1939, *Oil, 105" x 157",* Department of the Interior Building, Washington, DC.

Bureau of Indian Affairs: Indian & Soldier, Maynard Dixon, 1939, *Oil, 105" x 157",* Department of the Interior Building, Washington, DC.

Mail Coach Attacked by Bandits, William Palmer, 1937, *Oil, 7'x 13',* William Jefferson Clinton Federal Building (Old Post Office), Washington, DC.

and cleaned-up light of the present where they no longer posed a threat to the settlers but were brothers on the land. The self-taught artist eschews the heavier regionalism of American scene painting and takes on a more radiant light along with static pose and simplified space, recalling the more abstract style used by the Native Indian. The elegant, deeply resonant coloring and reduced form give a monumental feel to the figures and a distance to the simplified background. This is far cry from William C. Palmer's murals for the New

Post Office (now the William Jefferson Clinton Federal Building) in which frontiersmen's scalps as well as the mail were in extreme danger, as we shall see further along. It is interesting that these works were contemporary with one another, yet expressed vastly differing views of the Native American.

Popular also were themes of present-day economic and social events. Among the more specifically American were issues of race. Here in the art of the mural, a powerful voice was found.

Mitchell Jamieson, for example, created a mural for the Department of the Interior showing black artist Marian Anderson's 1939 concert at the Lincoln Memorial, a politically charged event that followed the Daughters of the American Revolution's refusal to allow Anderson to give a concert in their Constitution Hall, and First Lady Eleanor Roosevelt's subsequent resignation from the DAR. There are few better examples of the country coming to grips with the civil rights of its citizens than this

Covered Wagon Attacked by Indians, **William Palmer, 1937,** *Oil, 7' x 13',* William Jefferson Clinton Federal Building (Old Post Office), Washington, DC.

Insular Possessions Virgin Islands, **James Newell, 1939,** *Oil, 109" x 235",* Department of the Interior Building, Washington, DC.

depiction of intolerance overcome by art and heart!

The accomplishments of black Americans were also lauded in the darkly mysterious murals of Millard Sheets placed prominently in the new Interior Department's Grand Stair Hall.

The nation's distant territories and their peoples were addressed in pictures by James Michael Newell, Gifford Beal, and others.

Certainly, the full spectrum of America's territorial possessions from the blue-white light of the arctic circle to the yellow sun of the tropics were typical of the quasi-educational and scenic murals made for the

An Incident in Contemporary Life, Mitchell Jamieson, 1943, *Oil, 148" x 82"*, Department of the Interior Building, Washington, DC.

RELIGION

Religion, **Millard Owen Sheets,** 1939, *Oil, 107" x 77",* Department of the Interior Building, Washington, DC.

Department of the Interior.

At the Department of Justice, it was the civil rights of all Americans, regardless of race and gender, that were represented on almost every suitable surface, public or otherwise.

Arguably the most exciting imagery was created for the Postal Service, with murals illustrating the dangers and hardships in getting the mail delivered, as well as contemporary themes such as those painted by Alfred D. Crimi and Reginald Marsh on the processing and sorting of the mail, rendered in what I like to call "postal realism." The Section commissioned murals and sculptures not only for the capital's buildings but also for 1,100 post offices across the country.

In a sense, then, these murals were political as well as an aesthetic statement. They were not designed to stir the people but to ignite a feeling of pride. Social progress and stability were the key visual cues. We can see this aptly painted by Lithuanian-born Ben Shahn in his multi-panel mural, *The Meaning of Social Security*, which hangs in the lobby of the Department of Health and Human Services, also known as the Wilber J. Cohen Building in DC.

In showing the accomplishments of the New Deal, they serve as a voice for the various departments and segments of the federal government.

It should be noted that along with all this national enthusiasm and pride of place, the artists themselves would be paid and publicized. The program also helped some artists, such as Candido Portinari, reach new audiences beyond their own ethnic background by giving them a high-profile public platform for their work.

The Arts, Millard Owen Sheets, 1939, *Oil, 107" x 77",* Department of the Interior Building, Washington, DC.

Making and Placing the Murals

A mural painting commissioned by the Section on Fine Arts usually tended to be oil on canvas, but the fresco technique, though more trying, was also used.

There are two common ways of making the oil-on-canvas mural. The work could be painted on canvas stretched tight around a wooden structure or support called stretchers, and then the entire panel affixed to a wall. Another and more convenient way would be to affix the canvas directly to the wall after it had been completed without any frame or support, making it somewhat permanent. Since most of the murals were done in the latter fashion, they have become semi-permanent fixtures to the wall. For this method the artist would attach the canvas to the wall of the studio and paint directly from his approved sketches and colored renderings previously submitted to the Section.

Allowances would be made for whatever inconsistencies in the wall surface were encountered and sometimes potentially disastrous color schemes could be worked out in accordance with the general view of the building interior.

Some of the best paintings, such as those in the main stair and great hall at the Department of Justice Building, were created using the fresco technique. The most difficult technique to restore or remove, the pigments—usually a water-based paint—are applied directly to the wall that has been coated with wet plaster. The artist has to

The Meaning of Social Security, Ben Shahn, 1941, *Oil, detail*, Wilbur J. Cohen Federal Building, Washington, DC.

The Meaning of Social Security, Ben Shahn, 1941, *Oil, detail*, Wilbur J. Cohen Federal Building, Washington, DC.

The Discovery of Gold, **Candidio Portinari, 1939,** *Tempera,* Library of Congress, John Adams Building, Washington, DC.

Studio with a mural on a temporary stretcher.

Fresco painting in process.

Fresco painting in process.

View of hall, with floor-to-ceiling placement of murals. Department of the Interior Building, Washington, DC.

paint on site and work quickly with just enough paint to cover specified areas for that day. There is only a given amount of time within which to work before the paint and plaster dries and the surface becomes permanent.

Obviously, due to its difficult nature, this classic technique was used not as often in these murals, but similar effects of direct painting could be achieved by using the secco technique. In fact, this was the technique most favored by the Native American artists when doing murals for the Department of the Interior

With the secco technique of painting, the artist prepared a full-size unfinished sketch or cartoon on paper. The cartoons were usually traced onto brown paper and then perforated where the lines were, then taped across the wall that was to be painted. After being secured, the artist or his assistants would come with a small pouch of powdered charcoal and cover the perforations, transferring the work directly to the plaster as an outline for the artist. This technique is also used in fresco painting, though with wet plaster. The artist then paints directly on the wall.

Most of the time, the mural work was done in the studio of the artist. When finished and approved by the Section, the murals were rolled, shipped, and then mounted to the wall. The artists had to adjust their designs to fit spaces they might never see and overcome obstacles to compositions such as a doorway or a water fountain.

This and other issues involved in the creation of the mural could make the process long and arduous. A new building's architect could be somewhat nebulous in terms of articulating where artwork was going to be placed. It was up to the artist to determine how the composition itself had to be broken up to adjust with various wall inconsistencies.

Oftentimes a winning design did not fit the actual space or had to be reconsidered due to a lack of communal working between the architect and artist.

The architect's specs might indicate some decoration but in many sites it was an arbitrary choice and made without consultation. The situation made for tight compositions and difficulties for the mural's creator.

In some of the less prestigious locales, a lack of communication between architect and artist could lead to disharmonious color and other design issues. Colors of marble might clash with the main hue of the mural, for example, or the wall might happen to have a door in its middle.

Elevator lobby with mural. Federal Building and US Courthouse, Albuquerque, NM.

A mural that has had to be fitted around a door opening.

Often the physical space allotted was not entirely suitable. At times, the murals had to fit to walls never really intended to contain paintings. What might have been thought of as fill on the wall plane by the architect was a different matter for the Section, where it was hoped that, while waiting to get one's stamps, for example, one's spirit would rise spurred by the visual drama played out overhead.

There could be the added attraction of some door or opening cut into the picture plane (the surface of a painting). This difficulty of an interrupted narrative was not uncommon and usually was handled successfully by the artist. Great skill was needed to carry off a painting in a sometimes-hostile physical space and make the artwork look like a seamless part of the overall design.

A good example of an artist working past these obstacles is seen at the US Courthouse and Federal building in Albuquerque, New Mexico. Here, the artist had to allow not only for two elevator banks but also for a pair of large openings that create a problematic surface for a mural. In a wild portrayal of cowboys and Indians, bright in color and flat in depth, the resulting effect is more like a large stained-glass window. In color and form it is a wonderful example of the art of the West inter-

preted through the eyes of the New Deal, and it gives the lobby space a sense of importance as well as delight.

The disconnect between architect and artist was not always the case, however. In the Department of Justice Building, one of the first important and high-profile commissions awarded by the Section, it is obvious both architect and designer thought long and hard on how the work of art would integrate into the general scheme.

In more complex spaces, such as the DOJ Building, where walls were broken by columns and pilasters, the artist could deftly cut his compositions into a series of moments or vignettes, continuous with the total idea. Such details regarding the space, in the early commissions, were not given and changes would have to be made after the fact. The situation was remedied when the Section and its approval process decided to ask for color renditions. Artists were then given the general tone of the space, which would ensure that there would be unity with the interior.

The Submission Process

The Section required that a series of steps be followed to ensure that the finished works' final appearance was within the parameters set throughout both the selec-

tion as well as the actual painting process. Marlene Park and Gerald Markowitz's wonderful *Democratic Vistas: Post Offices and Public Art in the New Deal* explains the byzantine process of selection in some detail:

All artists who worked for the Section had to sign a contract committing them to several stages of preparatory work. Any large representational painting involves preliminary studies, but because of the great difference between the scale of preliminary and finished work for a mural, this stage is a more crucial one. In the first stage the artist submitted a black and white sketch and a color sketch on a scale of 1 inch equals 1 foot. In the second, the cartoon—a black and white drawing of the actual size of the finished work. And finally the third, the finished painting. The artist would receive a third of his or her fee at each of the three stages: when the Section officials approved the color sketch and a contract was signed, when they received a photograph and approved the cartoon in writing, and when they approved a photograph of the installed mural. Artists won competitions based on the color sketch. If they received one of the secondary commissions, they first had to submit black and white sketches for approval of both subject matter and design. The artist usu-

Law Versus Mob Violence, John Steuart Curry, year? Fifth-floor lobby Department of Justice Building, Washington, DC.

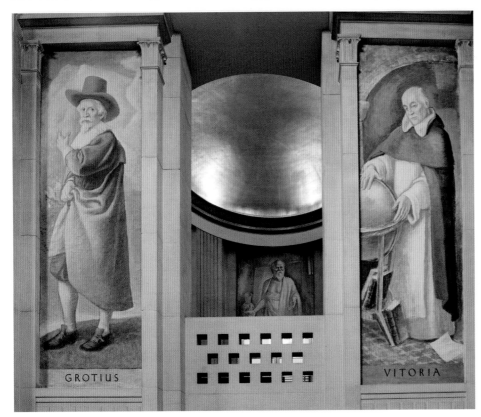

Hugo Grotius and Francisco de Vitoria, Boardman Robinson, 1937, *Oil, 12' x 4',* Department of Justice Building, Washington, DC.

ally submitted four ideas of which the Section chose one.

Starting with a black-and-white as well as a color sketch, the artist would draw out the design of the painting, which would indicate the general layout and placement of the figures as well as indicate the relationships and harmonies of the colors.

The pencil and color sketch could be as reductive or exacting as the artist felt it needed to be to best express his or her idea and the theme. Some artists chose to be cursory in the visual description and indicated the most general of layout designs, while others might paint a fairly complete rendition of their idea in all its details and form. Though the color sketch was most important in establishing the basic harmonies and look of the work, it was not necessarily the exact image that would be painted but a clear step to help the jury visualize the final idea. The size reduced for ease of viewing, the jury received a more finished view of the idea. This method would show how the artist intended to deal

The submission process for commissioned artwork: reviewing the colored sketches.

with the theme chromatically as well as solve whatever problems the wall presented.

The sketches would have indicated where and how cuts or interruptions would be dealt with in the mural. After it was approved, the artist would then make his full-size cartoon or mock-up, which was basically something he could work from to visualize and finalize the scale and adjust relationships of the figures to one another. It was the full-size mock-up, in black and white, that ultimately decided whether the mural was accepted or not. It was perhaps the most scrutinized element by the committee. At full size any and all details that might be of visual importance could be examined for correctness. Once the approval of this stage had passed, the artist created the actual oil painting and was paid accordingly. To quote from *Democratic Vistas* once more:

During the entire process the Section applied the greatest importance to the color sketch on the basis of which the competitions were judged and the contracts signed. In fact the colored sketch was the only stage at which the Section routinely saw the artists original work rather than a photograph.

This small-scale fully colored and rendered version of what the artist intended the mural to look like enabled the Section to endorse moving further with the full-scale cartoon drawing. It is interesting to note that the colored sketch was kept as the property of the Section and one is lucky, outside of the bureaucracy, to come across these rarely preliminary layouts that were sometimes later discarded.

As so much importance was placed on the colored sketch the artist naturally made sure that the narrative was as clear and

complete as possible. Once the sketch in color was approved, the contract was signed and the artist could move on whether or not he or she had seen the actual space allotted for it.

It was a slow and arduous process that in the end left little room for failure or disappointment with the end result.

After being completed and shown to the jury charged with its approval, the artist drew in charcoal a full-size cartoon, or mock-up, of the finished composition. This large-scale tonal or linear study allowed the artist to judge the planning and make sure the more important elements worked at full scale. It was a very critical part of the process as everything that would be right or wrong with the composition could be easily seen at this size. Elements that seemed insignificant at the smaller scale could suddenly be pushed into the spotlight

Desert, Nicolai Cikovsky, 1938, *Oil, 92" x 68",* Department of the Interior Building, Washington, DC.

stages and approval processes had a curbing effect on their creativity. I feel that this process of setting the theme in finality helped to give many of the works that particular weighty monumentality that we have come to identify with the New Deal and its art. The work produced, functioned, and looked exactly as was asked of it.

Even today, these murals continue to impress. Their themes of conservation or national parks and landscape, for example, are still alive in form and color. Their inspirational quality is as powerful today as ever. Seeing them, one can only wonder why they fell into neglect visually.

A National Legacy

Why is it that this once lauded and beautiful work has been allowed to hang in the shadows for so long unknown and unloved?

Part of the problem might be that with the passing of time and changing tastes, buildings were remodeled or worse, removed. The perception of what the murals represented changed. As time and grime gradually covered the already mellow colors, the paintings faded into the background as well as obscurity in the lens of art history. Through the rise of modernism, these works and the buildings that did survive were deemed terribly recherché, forgone conclusions of a past tense in art and design.

Only through the dedication of the GSA and its arts programs were many of the best preserved, especially in the capitol district, in the settings they were painted for.

In the vast Stewart Lee Udall Department of the Interior Building the insistent vanishing point of the central corridors is, as we have noted earlier, relieved and enlivened by some of the greatest and least-known names in American twentieth-century painting, as well some of the most beautiful and important examples of the genre. These formidable signifiers of time and history still dialogue easily in color and design. I have been there and have noted the looks of interest and pride in the art by the people who work for the government every day. Many of the buildings we have talked about are now altered or the original wall space is now cluttered with signs and counters, but in these DC federal buildings

and judged right or wrong for a particular location. This drawing, little more than a linear outline, was then used for transferring the image to the canvas, but it could also be quite complete. A cartoon allows one to see the scale and the details clearly. The paper piece could be hung high in the studio and lit as closely as possible to the what the lighting conditions might be at the chosen site, thus giving the painter an idea of what needed emphasis or had to be enlarged.

After this full-size drawing was further approved, usually by photographs, the artist would punch holes in all the major

outlines and then with powdered graphite or charcoal in a little cotton bag, pounce it over the outlines, transferring the drawing and its main compositional forms to the prepared canvas. The artist could then proceed to paint the picture, as its main outlines as well as most of the details and imagery were now in their proper place on the canvas. Many of the artists, especially those who worked in a more spontaneous and direct manner when working at their easels, found the exacting process to be unnecessary. In the end, they did what was required, though some of the more contemporary, younger artists felt all of the

Fighting Forest Fire, **Ernest Fiene, 1938**, *Oil, 92" x 68",* Department of the Interior Building, Washington, DC.

National Park Service, North Country, **Gifford Beal**, **1941**, *Oil, 105" x 224"*, William Jefferson Clinton Federal Building (Old Post Office), Washington, DC.

National Park Service, Tropical Country, **Gifford Beal**, **1941**, *Oil, 105" x 224"*, Department of the Interior Building, Washington, DC.

the lucky viewer can see the style intact.

The Interior Building is a behemoth of limestone and marble that covers an area of two blocks and is at every corner and turn stocked with visual surprises. This great storehouse of civic art still functions as a huge working office building for the government. Within the regimented façades are a series of public spaces and offices that show off the endeavors of the Treasury's Section for Fine Arts program and demon-

strate the astute choices that were made to decorate it and its neighbors.

Spanning the far end of the southern wall of the lobby floor is an enormous William Gropper mural, *Construction of the Dam*, painted in 1940. Here, on a huge scale (107 by 392 inches) in oil on canvas is pure WPA New Deal art at its peak. The viewer is almost invited to join in on the work; only the sound of the jackhammer missing from the scene. The composition

is focused on what in itself is almost an abstraction: the lifting of a huge semicircular section of pipe that dwarfs the workers and extends its powerful imagery right out of the picture plane and into the actual space.

Workers strain to coax the huge section into place in a complex arrangement that parallels the efforts of the government to set the country back on track. The idea of saving water and reclamation almost takes

The Building of a Dam, William Gropper, 1936, *Oil, 105" x 340",* Department of the Interior Building, Washington, DC.

a back seat to this national pride in accomplishment. The mural is noteworthy in the tripartite division that was used to fill the space yet allow for the continuation of the pilasters that line the corridor.

We see the same straining and lifting in the Gropper mural as we do in the Reginald Marsh fresco *Unloading the Mail,* painted for the New Post Office, where, instead of a beam, it is a sack of mail being lifted, but the message is the same—*Do it for America!* Through the many murals, placed strategically at opposing ends of what would be an endless perspective, one is afforded relief through color and storytelling. We are literally made a part of these pictures and, standing in front, one does become almost a member of the cast. The actual size as well as the subject is grand but the mural is mindful of the human viewer and the ordinary, now imbued with dignity.

The artists were paid according to the size and importance of the job. For example, William Gropper was paid just over $5,000 for his mural, by contract, which was about the average for this scale and his prominence. I would say that this mural painted in 1939 ranks with the most important works of his career and might be his most ambitious. This mechanized, industrialized vision of New Deal America with regards to land conservation and the reclamation of natural resources was the most popular theme in many of the new buildings.

At the Department of Justice Building in Washington, DC, one finds perhaps the most grand and wonderfully integrated cycle of wall decorations produced during the entire New Deal. Here, the fresco technique was used in a number of prominent locations, most impressively in the Grand Stair to the library on the fifth floor. In George Biddle's *Society Freed Through Justice,* the artist was especially successful

in dividing the composition to fit the space. No matter how much the idea of justice pervades, though, one still is more aware of the sense of luxe. In fact, the entire decorative theme of its ceremonial space extends to the hallways where only a privileged few would ever have glimpsed the works.

Over the years the frescoes at Justice have mellowed. The colors, still rich, have softened with time. The harmonies still ring true, though, as the nature of the technique allows for this subtle change. Unlike oil on canvas, which needs a protective final coat, the fresco is impervious.

The Justice Department, along with its many murals and frescoes, is also home to an unusually large number of decorative wall panels and reliefs as well as a series of mosaics and tiles that beautify even the more purely utilitarian needs of the building. It is clear that the artists and the architect were able to work together within

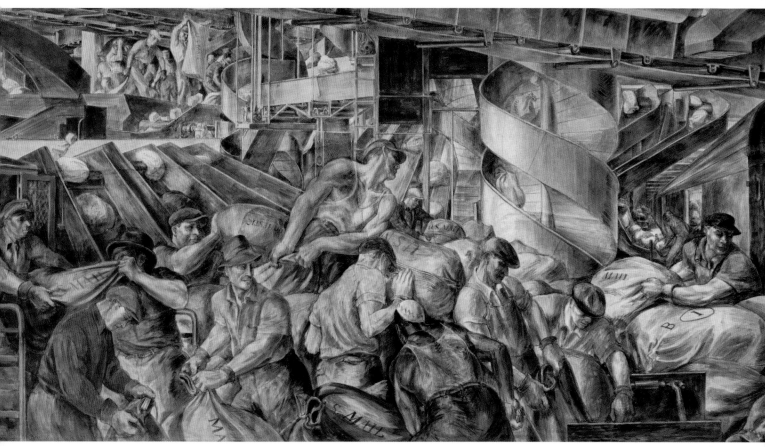

Sorting the Mail, Reginald Marsh, 1936, *Fresco, 6' 7" x 12' 6"*, William Jefferson Clinton Federal Building (Old Post Office), Washington, DC.

Unloading the Mail, Reginald Marsh, 1936, *Fresco, 6' 7" x 12' 6"*, William Jefferson Clinton Federal Building (Old Post Office), Washington, DC.

Society Freed Through Justice, George Biddle, 1936, *Fresco, 13' x 44'*, Department of Justice Building, Washington, DC.

Justice of the Plains: The Movement Westward, John Steuart Curry. 1938, *Oil*, Department of Justice Building, Washington, DC.

Spirit of Justice, Paul Jennewein, 1933, *Cast aluminum,* Department of Justice Building, Washington, DC.

the interior spaces to make a harmonious whole statement.

Speaking of Justice and her iconography, C. Paul Jennewein's *Spirit of Justice* statue, commissioned in 1933, had a period of notoriety when the George W. Bush Administration had curtains put in front of the statue after Atty. Gen. John Ashcroft stood in front of the bare-breasted beauty in all her glory during a televised press conference. For the duration of the Bush administration, Lady Justice remained draped under a blue cloth of shame like some branded fallen woman during the puritanical times of our founding. She is now fully exposed with her partner, *Majesty of Law*, also in gleaming aluminum and who had also been similarly draped.

As important as the paintings are the sculptures and bas-reliefs are used everywhere in the capital. Perhaps the most famous of these is Michael Lantz's *Man Controlling Trade* statue at the very base of the Federal Triangle at the Department of Trade. A man holds a rearing horse, and in its muscularity, the statue provides a substantial and sensual portrayal of strength, mirroring in some ways the tension of the country and the world during those troubled times.

The US Post Office commissioned a number of cast aluminum statues as well.

Another artist working in the fresco technique was Henry Varnum Poor, a noted ceramicist and painter who was used to working on wet surfaces upon which to apply color. For these specific talents, Poor was called by the Section to fresco ten panels in a long, ample corridor leading to the various private chambers of the Justice Department. The panels he created are set into recessed niches and surround large entry doors to the private chambers. The sense of excitement one feels upon entering this rather long hall is quite delightful. An otherwise boring space was turned into more than just a corridor; it worked as a reminder of the meaning of the building. The *Washington Post*, in its review of the new building, noted this particular set of murals to be extremely successful in color and in meaning, and an exemplary piece of civic art and decoration.

The tour de force of the Department of Justice has to be its Grand Stair Hall. This

Man Controlling Trade, Michael Lantz, 1942, *Granite*, Federal Trade Commission Building, Washington, DC.

astonishing work is adjacent to and opens to the vestibule of the Justice Department Library. Here, John Steuart Curry's murals, beneath the silvered and vaulted ceiling, reflect the sometimes disturbing aspects of justice in America. These were themes the New Deal and PWA especially wished to address in a time of discontent and disparity. Curry's depictions of Justice as protector and enforcer offer a theme that was very important to the New Deal: Justice for All was doubly encoded in both the structure and its art.

All of the sixty or so murals in the Justice Department have something to do with jurisprudence. As an ensemble, they are ranked with the crème de la crème of the entire WPA art program, along with those of the Department of the Interior and the postal department's wonderful paintings.

Color and Stone

It is only fitting since the idea of the WPA and the postal service go hand-in-hand that we should show here more of the many murals painted for the system. Besides the works painted for the DC building, art was also being created for the hundreds of other new buildings scattered across the country. The US Post Office had a presence in every town, city, and state across the union. It was this widespread visibility that made it a suitable and desirable program within which the arts Section could exercise its responsibility. From the canyons of Manhattan to the Grand Canyon of Colorado, the local post office was a ubiquitous presence and one whose walls presented countrywide stages for the American scene to be painted out.

The artist as we have seen had to fit his work of art within a given space that might or might not have been thought of as a suitable location for a painting. At times,

works made to fit within a series of blind arches, or niches, as we have seen in Binghamton, New York, had to be composed by the artist to fit comfortably. This made-to-fit quality was a result of the artist not having any control over the shape of the space where the Section authorized a mural. Rarely was the intended space seen in person, and it was subject to whatever changes might occur during the final phases of building construction. Placement could be indicated anywhere but usually at either the narrow space above the postal counter, where the painting worked as a frieze, or at either end of the postal facility where the work was apt to be interrupted by a door or utilitarian counter.

In the end, there was no problem that could not be solved by the ingenuity and skill of the artist. As noted, most of these paintings were done in the artists' studios on canvas and later affixed to the walls. In Washington, DC, the New Post Office

Justice and Industry, **Henry Varnum Poor, 1939,** *Fresco (Door Surround),* Department of Justice Building, Washington, DC.

War and Peace, **Anton Refregier, 1941,** *Oil,* Rincon Annex Post Office, San Francisco, CA.

NORTH SOUTH

Art Deco Ships, *Oil*, Rincon Annex Post Office, San Francisco, CA.

commissioned oil on canvas as well as fresco for a cycle of paintings in sets of two per artist to illustrate the history and workings of the department. For the most part their style was realist and solid, but there were also aesthetic tendencies that spoke more closely to the new modern art of America as well.

One of the more interesting artists working with less-specific form was Anton Refregier with his mural *War and Peace* at the Rincon Annex Post Office near the Embarcadero in San Francisco. The simplified shapes and flat colors make his painting very close to both the decorative qualities of the art deco and the multi-dimensionality of the moderns. Looking at the mural we can see how comfortably it blends the semi-deco, semi-abstract, and streamlined into the forms that give it a very moderne feel.

The delivery of the mail and its processing are central to the whole series of murals authorized by the Section for the US Post Office. By giving the subject either a historical or contemporary location in time, the artist created almost cinematic imagery to enliven the tasks of posting a letter.

Style Follows Function

Though close on the heels of art deco, the New Deal murals managed to stay away from the geometric and stylized jazziness of that style. Where something close to the zig and zag of art deco did appear in New Deal work, it was usually in a decorative motif or an architectural element in the form of exterior carved details.

In the end, all of these decorations, for they were commissioned to decorate, had to follow a form. No matter how difficult or how unsuitable the allotted space for

the artwork, the artist solved the problem. All of the paintings and murals are examples of a style that aimed to be distinctly American, a nebulous sort of idea given the many possibilities. In this respect, the art was realist and redundant in its story of the homeland—tonal and earthy, with an emphasis on the everyday. It was a more conservative form of the narrative ideas of the popular social realist poster, which at times, it could resemble.

During the '30s, there were as many "isms" in art as there were "alphabet soup" organizations in the New Deal. There were European-influenced avant-garde abstractions, but for most people, modern art referred to art that did not have gods and goddesses. Psychological and abstract art that needed interpretation would not work for the WPA— it was too cerebral and more at home in a museum or gallery. The only WPA artists who came close to this sort of style were Refregier, Rockwell Kent, and Eugene Savage, who all worked with semi-streamlined forms and flatness.

In paintings such as the ones at San Francisco's Rincon Annex Post Office or the set of Savage murals in Washington we get as deco as I have seen aside from murals that would have been commissioned for non-public and non-governmental concerns such as department stores and the lobbies of the new skyscrapers.

Savage's murals stand out as some of the most interesting in their use of bright color and the change from illusionistic space to a more floating world of semi-streamlined abstractions. They form a sort of panoply of postal integrity, uniting all of the architectural and symbolic elements in a way slightly more reminiscent of the typical art deco, save for the less stylized elements.

In popular culture, where capital and capitalism were building, only the most fashionable and least controversial imagery would be allowed. Big business was not interested in the social justice and morality of the WPA art. The private sector embraced deco for its languorous and even louche style that did not suggest the idea of "work" in any way.

WPA art, by definition, concerned itself with the plight of the working man, social

Mail Service in the Tropics, Rockwell Kent, 1937, *Oil, 7' x 13'*, William Jefferson Clinton Federal Building (Old Post Office), Washington, DC.

Mail Service in the Arctic, Rockwell Kent, 1937, *Oil, 7' x 13'*, William Jefferson Clinton Federal Building (Old Post Office), Washington, DC.

injustice, and racial inequality, as well as the mechanization of the country. "Thematic relief" could be found in the scenic vistas that were called for by various departments and these works featured wide expanses of sky, clouds, and, yes, workers toiling in the fields. The artists portrayed the grandness of our continent and the American movement west. There were plenty of themes to go around but when it came to addressing America's social conscious, especially in regard to racial injustice, Washington, DC, held back no punches to make clear its total commitment to the cause of change.

With thought-provoking works such as Mitchell Jamieson's *An Incident in Contemporary Life* and Millard Sheets's four-pan-

MESSENGER OF SYMPATHY AND LOVE   SERVANT OF PARTED FRIENDS   CONSOLER OF THE LONELY   BOND OF THE SCATTERED FAMILY   ENLARGER OF THE COMMON LIFE

Messenger of Sympathy and Love, **Eugene Savage**, **1937**, *Oil, 7' x 13'*, William Jefferson Clinton Federal Building (Old Post Office), Washington, DC

CARRIER OF NEWS AND KNOWLEDGE   INSTRUMENT OF TRADE AND INDUSTRY   PROMOTER OF MUTUAL ACQUAINTANCE   OF PEACE AND OF GOOD WILL   AMONG MEN AND NATIONS

Carrier of News and Knowledge, **Eugene Savage**, **1937**, *Oil, 7' x 13'*, William Jefferson Clinton Federal Building (Old Post Office), Washington, DC.

el *The Negro's Contribution in the Social and Cultural Development of America*, both for the Department of the Interior, and murals on religion and science that are elegiac yet somber in tone, art is telling a story. That sense of total detachment one can get from purely abstract work is not here; instead the viewer feels a vital connection and attachment to the story. This is what happens when art works and when art has a story to tell. And throughout the federal government and especially in the buildings of the Federal Triangle in Washington, DC, all of these elements came together to illustrate the New Deal.

Contemporary Justice and Woman, Emil Bisttram, 1937, *Tempera* , Department of Justice Building, Washington, DC.

Afterword: A Call to Arts

The explicit demands made upon the WPA artists as well as its architects and designers left a legacy of aesthetic accomplishment, as well as a time capsule of the American scene between the wars. The importance of these works both then and today is clear: They give us a glimpse into our past and illuminate the road we traveled—sometimes not a bright one, but

always hopeful, determined, and American.

These murals along with the doors and decorative grilles, mosaics, and architec-tural details all added up to the sum total of the WPA visually and aesthetically. They inform and show us the design and archi-tecture of the time as well as the art, both decorative and fine, of America during the '30s. Indeed, they represent the very best

Country Post, **Doris Lee**, 1938, *Oil, 7' x 13' 6"*, William Jefferson Clinton Federal Building (Old Post Office), Washington, DC.

of the period's public and civic art and design.

In general much of the WPA sculptural work was more a part of the architecture and was always site-specific, designed to fully integrate with the building or interior. Their function was to give some relief to the oftentimes repetitive expanses of wall or serve as spandrels and lintels within the architect's scheme. Although they are additive, just like the murals, they tend to be more integrated into the design rather than afterthoughts of the designers. It is for this that I included examples of bas-relief and sculpture in the first part of the book, as it dealt with the architectonic issues of the design and it is impossible to see the structure without its relief.

From necessity, and despair, American art found its voice through the WPA, one that could be heard outside of the museum. These works of art scattered throughout America were testimony to the New Deal's intent to see the country through the eyes of its citizens.

It is our great fortune that these American treasures, historic and aesthetic, have been dutifully kept and preserved under the auspices of the Department of the In-

terior and the GSA. After World War II, many murals and works of art, as well as the buildings they inhabited, were deemed obsolete or old-fashioned and in some cases destroyed. We are lucky that the GSA did try to remove and preserve the paintings where possible. These works are not currently on view but are maintained in pristine state awaiting their resurrection in some future public space that can accommodate them.

While some of the art and architecture remains in place, primarily in Washington, DC, much of it is no longer accessible. Many of the works from the years between the World Wars that show the highest caliber of American painting unfortunately are not easily viewed by the public. Most, if not all, of the federal buildings that they decorate are rarely open to the public. Since the terrible rise of the Age of Terrorism, no longer can just anyone gain entrance to these buildings without official clearance, and thus these paintings and other works of art remain prisoners in gilded cages.

It has been my hope that along with a renewed interest in the civic architecture of the time, I could also ignite a fire with regard to interest in the paintings and

sculpture created to adorn these buildings. All of the paintings shown here, as well as many more similar works of WPA-commissioned art, are now virtually incommunicado in their settings. Certainly one can find other works by the artists in various collections, public and private, but that particular subject and theme, its particular intent and meaning, is no longer accessible. While we have access to digital images of the art, an appreciation of the scale and physical placement is no longer possible. That door is for now closed to us.

The feeling that I get when I see these works is precisely what was hoped for by the Section that commissioned the art. At the risk of sounding maudlin, I felt good whenever I had the opportunity to stand in front of one of these joint efforts between the arts and the government. I enjoyed their details and their stories. They informed of their time. Never did I find them to be intimidating, pompous, or doctrinaire.

Save for the Ben Shahn murals and a handful of other works, most are not what we can really consider Great Art. But they all show some understanding of their subjects and, at the least, can be seen as good painting.

Petroleum Industry: Distribution and Use, **Edgar Britton, 1939,** *Oil, 111" x 235",* Department of the Interior Building, Washington, DC.

Petroleum Industry: Production, **Edgar Britton, 1939,** *Oil, 111" x 235",* Department of the Interior Building , Washington, DC.

Above all, the art and architecture of the New Deal still does the job it set out to do. It is real American art—sometimes a dry and sober look at its subject, yet excit-ing enough in spirit to stir patriotic feeling and emotion.

It helps us see and reflect upon a piv-otal time in our country's history and appreciate the greatness and lasting impact of FDR's New Deal.

Acknowledgments

Sculpture over the door of the Federal Trade Commission Building, Washington, DC.

This book could not have been made without the wonderful and beautifully accurate photographs of Carol Highsmith, the architectural photographer for the GSA in Washington, DC, whose collection, The Carol Highsmith archives, is part of the Library of Congress archives and was of constant and always pleasurable use.

Her willingness to make wonderful images available and to lend her eye to make my points was invaluable.

Thank you also to the Library of Congress for the use of their Historic Buildings archive, another weekly mined source; their personal assistance both in Washington and online was always quick and helpful. I am so lucky to have learned the ropes of being an author with their guidance—so lucky for me!

I am grateful to Christine Ewing, who, with the wonderful people at the GSA, helped me make this book come true.

I owe the GSA so much. The entire government staff was always there to give a hand.

I must thank my publisher, Pete Schiffer, who liked my novice idea enough to offer me this chance to share my love of this period with the many others who feel this special time and place in architectural history has been wrongfully neglected. My editor, Catherine Mallette, helped me through this difficult first book. I am not able to say enough kind words about her patience and care and her superb edit of my oft-wandering words.

To Gloria and Bob Fox—great architects and designers, who got me through my trips to Washington.

To Illianna van Meerteran, and to Terrance Boylen, who went out of his way to show me the right way.

To my friend and tech man Sean Thompson, who showed me how!

And to my dear friend Carolyn, whose constant nudging and truthful objectivity was a priceless gift. She was always there to pick me up when I needed help.

Bibliography

Grossman, Elizabeth Greenwell. *The Civic Architecture of Paul Cret*. New York: Cambridge University Press, 1996.

Kennedy, Roger G. *When Art Worked: The New Deal, Art, and Democracy*. New York: Rizzoli International Press, 2009.

Luebke, Frederick C. *A Harmony of the Arts: The Nebraska State Capitol*. Lincoln, NE: University of Nebraska Press, 1996.

Park, Marlene and Gerald E. Markowitz. *Democratic Vistas: Post Offices and Public Art in the New Deal*. Philadelphia: Temple University Press, 1984.

Rydell, Robert W. and Laura B. Schiavo. *Designing Tomorrow: America's World's Fairs of the 1930s*. New Haven: Yale University Press, 2010.

Schrenk, Lisa D. *Building a Century of Progress: The Architecture of Chicago's 1933–34 World's Fair*. Minneapolis: University of Minnesota Press, 2007.

Weber, Eva. *American Art Deco*. Greenwich, CT: Brompton Book Corporation, 1984.

Wilson, Richard Guy, Dianne H. Pilgrim, and Dickran Tashjian. *The Machine Age in America: 1918–1941*. Brooklyn Museum/Harry N. Abrams, 1986.

Building Index, by State
with Completion Dates and Architects